I AM MY MOTHER'S DAUGHTER

I AM MY MOTHER'S DAUGHTER

Wisdom on Life, Loss, and Love

DARA KURTZ

Mandel Vilar Press

This book is typeset in Filosofia OT 12/16. The paper used in this book meets the minimum requirements of ANSI/NISO Z39.48-1992 (R1997). ∞

Designed by Sophie Appel
Cover photos by iStock.com/whilerests and tete_escape/Shutterstock.com

Library of Congress Cataloging-in-Publication Data
(Prepared by The Donohue Group, Inc.)

Names: Kurtz, Dara, author.
Title: I am my mother's daughter : wisdom on life, loss, and love / Dara Kurtz.
Description: Simsbury, Connecticut : Mandel Vilar Press, [2020]
Identifiers: ISBN 9781942134657 | ISBN 9781942134664 (ebook)
Subjects: LCSH: Kurtz, Dara—Family. | Mothers and daughters. | Jewish women. | Cancer—Patients. | Loss (Psychology)
Classification: LCC HQ755.86 .K87 2020 (print) | LCC HQ755.86 (ebook) | DDC 306.8743—dc23
Printed in the United States of America
20 21 22 23 24 25 26 27 28 / 9 8 7 6 5 4 3 2 1

Mandel Vilar Press
19 Oxford Court, Simsbury, Connecticut 06070
www.americasforconservation.org | www.mvpublishers.org

To Mom, Grandma Margaret, and Grandma Millie:
I am blessed to be your daughter and granddaughter
and to have been loved by each of you. Thank you
for writing me beautiful letters full of timeless wisdom,
and for teaching me how to be a mom.

To my daughters, Zoe and Avi: Being your mom is a gift
I don't take for granted. You make my life fun
and meaningful, and I love how close we are.

CONTENTS

Contents

ACKNOWLEDGMENTS

To Jon, my NJB (nice Jewish boy), who has stayed by my side for over twenty-seven years: Thank you for your constant support, your level-headedness, and your unconditional love. Being with you has made my life better than I could have ever imagined. I'm especially grateful to you, Zoe, and Avi, for giving me permission to share our story.

To Dad: Thank you for raising me, right beside Mom. I cherish our time, our talks, and our deep friendship.

To my stepmother, Lois, and my in-laws, Suzy and Arthur: I am grateful to have you in my life. Thank you for always being there for me, and for loving me and treating me like your own daughter.

To my brother, Ari: I love our chats throughout the day, and I am incredibly grateful to have your love and friendship.

To David, Meggie, James, Sarah, Mila, and Theo: I enjoy our time together and traveling through life with you. Your friendship is a blessing in my life.

To my Richmond and Winston families: Thank you for your love and support, and for many meaningful memories. A special thanks to cousin Art for reading the first draft of my manuscript and for giving me the confidence to move forward with it.

Acknowledgments

To my mommy tribe, partners in crime, gym buddy, and walking friends; my camp, high school, and college friends; and the Tuesday Maj group: I am grateful to each of you.

To my podcast partner, Garth: I love our friendship, long talks, and not being judged for doing the podcast in my PJs on most days.

To Rich and Richie at Unimedia: Thanks for your willingness to always help me, your patience with my technology questions, and for your support.

To all of the strong and brave women I have met in the breast cancer world: Thank you for your friendship and love and for showing me what a warrior looks like.

To the followers of my blog, Crazy Perfect Life: Thank you for walking this path with me, for your constant support, and for inspiring me every day.

Finally, I am grateful to the amazing team at Mandel Vilar Press: To Robert Mandel for his guidance and support and for helping me make this the best book it could be; to my copyeditor, Mary Beth Hinton, who helped me think about things I might not have considered and was super patient when I kept making changes to the manuscript, giving her more work to do; to Sophie Appel, for designing a cover that was spot on and more pleasing than anything I could have imagined; and to Barbara Werden, production manager and designer, for keeping us on schedule and making sure the book design and format were just right.

I AM MY MOTHER'S DAUGHTER

INTRODUCTION

For most of my adult life, I've had a ziplock bag containing letters I received, from the first time I went to sleep-away camp until I graduated from college. The letters were from my parents and my grandparents, but mostly from my mom and two grandmothers. I learned many lessons from these strong Jewish women, who have each passed away. Many times over the past years I've longed to talk with them and hear what they think about the life I have created for myself. Living in a world without them has been among the greatest challenges of my adult life.

Though I knew where this bag was, I didn't have the courage to open it and reread the letters. I was fearful that reading them would bring back the grief I had worked so hard to overcome.

Because of an unexpected occurance, I finally opened the bag. I was shocked by what happened next. Rereading the letters, after so many years, brought me unanticipated peace, love, and a renewed connection to my mom and grandmothers. I gave myself permission to let go of the sadness I'd been holding onto since their deaths, and the experience transformed my life.

As a mom of two daughters, Zoe who is twenty and Avi who is seventeen, I try to pass on family traditions and wisdom, weaving the past with the future, making sure my daughters know who they are and where they came from. I want them to know about the special women who loved and raised me, and feel proud to call these women their family. I've learned that leaning into the past is best done through the lens of love, and as I unexpectedly discovered, through the handwritten word.

CHAPTER 1

You Never Know
What You Might Find
Stuffed in a Drawer

T here are moments in life that seem ordinary, and it's not until much later that we realize their significance. One such moment changed everything for me.

My daughter Zoe packed up to go back to school after winter vacation, the first time our family had spent a sizable chunk of time together since we took her for her first year of college back in August. The rest of us were still adjusting to life without seeing her every day. I was feeling a little sad about her leaving, even though she loved school and couldn't wait to get back.

It had been pure joy having her home for this first long break. During our time together we had enjoyed lazy mornings, talking while eating breakfast, taking long walks together, and binge-watching Netflix shows, including two seasons of *The Marvelous Mrs. Maisel*, to which I had become addicted.

While she was upstairs packing, I tried to distract myself because I didn't want to think about having to say good-bye. I didn't want her to have to deal with my emotions or feel guilty about leaving as she headed back to school for her second semester.

It amazed me to think that my daughter was a freshman in college. It didn't seem that long ago when I was the daughter leaving to go back to school. Zoe goes to a small school in North Carolina, only an hour away. She decided to go there because it's close to home, she fell in love with it the first moment she stepped onto the campus, and it happens to be over ten percent Jewish. Having grown up in North Carolina and been the only Jewish student in her grade at school, she was excited about this.

I had gone to the University of Alabama, over ten hours away, and I met my husband, Jon, there. He was an older NJB (nice Jewish boy). My parents were thrilled. While I've never been particularly religious, I was brought up to have a strong Jewish identity, and we raised our daughters the same way. I knew it had been hard on my mom that I was so far away, but I didn't realize what that felt like until I was a mom myself, having to say good-bye when my own daughter went off to college.

"Come into my room when you've finished packing," I called up to Zoe. "I'm getting dressed and you can talk to me while I straighten up my room."

"Okay," she said. "But, Mom, we really need to leave soon. We want to get back to school."

"I know, Zoe," I said. "Just come talk to me before you go." I've learned that the best way to move through hard good-byes is to have something to focus on other than the good-bye itself.

Zoe had a friend from school who had been visiting since New Year's Eve, and they both came into my room. I have two nice leather chairs in my bedroom, caramel colored with soft leather, and Zoe and her friend, Emma, sat down. Sitting in these chairs, my daughters and I have had beautiful conversations over the years.

When they were very young, our bed seemed to be the place where Zoe and Avi spent a lot of time. We read books, watched old TV shows like *The Brady Bunch*, talked, and laughed. On many nights when the girls were very young, the four of us fell asleep together, snuggled up tightly in a king-size bed, almost too squished to move. At the time, Jon and I often complained about this, wanting to have a solid night's sleep and a little more privacy. But we were often too tired at night to do anything about it. Plus, we knew it was a temporary situation. When my daughters were older, the chairs replaced snuggling up together in bed.

I had piles of laundry stacked up on an ottoman in my room, and shoes were everywhere. As I put the clothes away, Zoe and Emma talked with me about all the fun they were going to have back at school. They were excited about their new classes, seeing their friends, and a sorority rush that would happen soon after they returned. As we talked, Zoe opened the top drawer of the side table that sits between the two leather chairs, and started looking through the mess. While I'm usually good about keeping my house clean, I have my share of disorganized drawers that would make good projects for Marie Kondo.

As Zoe looked through the mess, including an unfinished knitting project, several orange-reddish yarn skeins, an old cell phone, and a computer cord, something caused her to stop.

"What's this?" she asked.

"I'm not sure," I said, not really paying attention. "Probably an old journal I need to get rid of."

"MOM!" Zoe exclaimed. "It's our mommy-daughter journal. The one we started when I was in middle school. OMG." She was smiling and almost bouncing up and down.

"It is?" I asked. I knew what she was talking about, even though I had not thought about that journal for years. I dropped the clean laundry and went over to see what Zoe was holding. She was right; it was our mommy-daughter journal, and I was equally excited about finding this treasure.

Zoe and I couldn't believe our good fortune, and as we celebrated our discovery, I explained to Emma what was going on and why we were getting so worked up over an old journal.

"We started this when Zoe was in middle school," I told Emma, who was watching us and smiling but didn't have a clue about what was going on. "It was a fun way for us to communicate with each other. We haven't seen this in years, and I had actually forgotten about it."

I started the mommy-daughter journals with each of my daughters in 2011 because I felt we needed a way to share our feelings without getting angry with one another. When Zoe was eleven and Avi was eight, there was a lot of bickering going on between all of us. They would get frustrated, I would get frustrated, and we would end up yelling at one another about something silly and insignificant. I've learned that words said in the heat of the moment can't be taken back, and can sting for a long time. In the journals we could share whatever was on our minds. Also, I knew that, if they were reading an entry I wrote to them, I was more likely to have their full attention, and I could put in writing how amazing I thought they were and boost their self-esteem.

When I first got the journals, I told them how excited I was to have a special book for each of them. The plan was for us to write to each other whenever we felt like it. It was going to be fun. I had bought two journals at T. J. Maxx that were identical except for the color. Zoe's had purple flowers on the cover and Avi's had burgundy flowers. Zoe and Avi couldn't wait to start. In those days they thought

I was a superhero, and they pretty much went along with whatever I suggested. We would write to one another in a journal, and then put it on the recipient's pillow. She would read it and respond, and so on. There weren't any rules and we didn't follow a schedule. It was there for us when we felt like using it.

With Emma watching us, we opened Zoe's mommy-daughter journal and began reading out loud. This was my first entry to Zoe:

. . . .

MOMMY-DAUGHTER JOURNAL ENTRY, 2011

Dear Zoe,

You are my precious little girl and I'm starting this journal with you with the intent to give it to you when you graduate from high school. I'm going to write in it each year, with a summary of the events for that year. I hope one day we can read this together and I can share with you as much about your childhood as you want to know. As you know, my mother was not able to be with me when I had you. There are so many things about my childhood I want to know, that I never thought to ask, until I had you. I hope this book will supply you with the answers to your questions, as you get older. I also want this to be a place you can go to share whatever is going on in your life. I will always do my best to help you work out whatever you're going through.

Family is the most important part of our life, and we hope you always remember that. I'm excited about us writing together. Remember, you can tell me anything. I love you so much,

Mom
. . . .

As we read this first entry, Zoe and I laughed.

"So much for giving this to you at graduation," I said. "I'm sorry."

"That would have been really cool," Zoe said. "But I'm glad we found it now."

We both looked at one another and Zoe squeezed my hand. A look passed between us.

Zoe's first entry to me was the following:

. . . .

MOMMY-DAUGHTER JOURNAL ENTRY, 2011

Mom,

Sometimes I feel like no-one likes me at school. I know I have some great friends, but that's like maybe three only. Maybe I'm exaggerating but I don't think I am. I know nobody would die to be my friend like some of the other girls. I don't want to switch schools or anything, and I love my education here. By the way, I'm scared that I'm not going to get honor roll. I'm scared if I don't get honor roll you will be angry with me. I don't want to throw it all away. Also, about Avi, sometimes she can be so annoying. You just say it's me, but it's not. It's Avi also. She does that face to me and yells and exaggerates a ton. She is too sensitive. I might <u>accidentally</u> fall over and she says I hit her. When that happens, my TV is gone for the night. Plus, when Avi does something bad she gets a "It's OK don't do it again." But, I lose TV immediately. I know she is only 8 1/2 but still she is sooo sneaky!! She has like the mind of a 5th grader and then she gets all "Mommy, it wasn't me," or "Mommy, I need help with my homework." I feel like I'm the bad guy. You and Daddy just don't understand.

*Back to the school thing. Please tell me what to do. I know
it's all part of growing up and that you had the same issue when
you were my age. I don't care. I need help! Please write back
quickly.*

Peace and love, Zoe

Zoe turned to me and we both laughed.

"That was a hard year," she said. "I really didn't have many friends."

"I know," I said. "But you got through it."

We both smiled because now Zoe is the kind of person who never meets a stranger and is like the Pied Piper when it comes to having friends. My journal response to her was the following:

MOMMY-DAUGHTER JOURNAL ENTRY, 2011

Dear Zoe,

*That's a hard one. It sounds to me like you're feeling like you
don't have any friends. I know we can figure this out together.
Think about your true friends, friends you can have fun with
and who love you for who you are. You don't have to try and
impress them. They like you for being Zoe. I know you don't think
it's a big deal to have 3 close friends, but it really is. Feel good
about that. It's the end of school and summer is right around
the corner. Everyone always gets sick of each other at the end of
the school year. Just try to hang in there for another week and*

then you will have a great summer break. Let's use the summer to expand your friend group. Let's pick a couple girls you would like to get to know better and invite them over. I know there are a lot of nice girls in your class and I'm sure they would love to get to know you better. I know you're working really hard right now and you will pull out honor roll. But if you don't we won't be angry. We just want good things for you. Just try your best! I know Avi isn't perfect. Just try to be the more mature big sister and walk away when she gets annoying. Always remember how much we love you and how special you are to us. You always have a friend in your family.

I love you, Mom

I had to pat myself on the back when I read that entry. "I gave good advice, don't you think?" I said to Zoe.

Zoe and I were holding hands as we read through the journal and had tears in our eyes. Reading her journal reminded me of the little girl she used to be. I hadn't thought about that little girl in a long time. I visualized a tall, skinny, smiling girl with braces and green and purple glasses. I missed that girl. Zoe and I were both laughing and smiling, and Emma was along for the ride.

Saying good-bye to Zoe wasn't as hard as I thought it would be. When the two girls headed back to school about an hour later, I was too happy about finding the journal to stay in a place of sadness. I went on with the day, thinking about years gone by and cherished memories. It's strange how you can have memories buried inside of you, waiting to emerge if the right trigger comes along. I wanted so much to call my mom and talk with her about how I, as a mom, had to let my own daughter leave. But I couldn't. She is no longer living.

Here is a letter my mom sent to me when I was at college:

. . . .

LETTER FROM MOM, 1990

Dearest Dara,

As always, it takes me a few days to get back into the swing of things when you go back to school. Let me say, Dara, that I loved having you home this summer. You were a delight to be with each day and I had fun with you. I hope by now you are situated in your dorm, that you have obtained your books, gone to all your classes, and are having fun. How are you? How is your roommate? I guess that I'm suggesting you communicate with us. We don't know anything (a typical response from a concerned Jewish Mother.) I am busy finishing up a few things in the house and I'm attending aerobic classes and plan to continue. Stay well!

Love, Mom
. . . .

The next morning, getting back into my normal routine after the holiday season, I kept thinking about the journal. It filled my heart with joy and happiness. It also made me think about my relationship with my mom, and I was wishing I had had something like a mommy-daughter journal with my mom. What I wouldn't do to have something I could put my hands on and read her words now. It had been almost twenty years since she passed away, and some of my memories were fading.

11

That's when I remembered all the letters I had saved throughout my childhood.

There were the ones my mom sent to me when I was at summer camp and college—like the one above. I had forgotten about them, even though I knew exactly where they were in my house. I could close my eyes and see the worn ziplock bag, waiting for me at the back of a drawer. Every time I had thought about opening the bag over the years, I had instead gone on with my life. It was easier this way. It was as if subconsciously I thought I could lock all my sadness inside the bag and keep it buried deep in a drawer.

Though I was afraid of reliving the pain of my loss, that walk down memory lane with Zoe made me inquisitive. Was I now ready to read the letters? What did they say? How would they make me feel?

I went to the drawer and opened it. Stuffed between old linens, the bag was there. I picked it up and saw the colored envelopes and the cute stickers used to seal them. I recognized the familiar handwriting. Then I put the plastic bag back in the drawer and closed it. I walked away.

"It's okay," I told myself. "You don't have to read them if you aren't ready. Plus, you've waited this long, what's a little more time? It doesn't matter." I tried not to judge myself for my lack of courage, but truth be told, I was a little disappointed in myself. I knew I really did want to know what the letters said. I was craving contact with my mom.

Hello, fear, there you are again. Fear, that four-letter word, can get in the way of reaching our full potential and taking advantage of all the opportunities that life has to offer. For so long, I put off read-ing the letters because of fear. I was focusing on the negative. I was holding myself back and preventing myself from experiencing this beautiful gift.

When I was a child, I thought we were rich. It wasn't until I was old enough to understand the value of all the "stuff" I coveted, that

I realized we weren't rich monetarily. Though we were comfortable, there were times when I felt the financial worries my parents carried. I knew what it felt like to want something and be told we couldn't afford it. I learned the value of hard work, of saving my money. And, while I might not have had as many pairs of Guess jeans or as many Forenza sweaters as I wanted, or taken some of the fancy vacations other kids talked about, I knew my family was rich in other ways. We had abundant love and respect for one another. As I've gotten older and matured, and met other people who didn't have these riches, I've come to realize how truly blessed I was. I understood that the best things in life don't come with a price tag and aren't sold in a store. They have to be felt. Like the undeniable and unconditional love I grew up having from my parents and grandparents.

I enjoy having many beautiful items and pieces of jewelry that belonged to my mom and grandmothers. I wear my favorites: a gold bracelet left to me by my grandma Margaret and a diamond necklace I never take off that was once worn by my grandma Millie and then my mom. But after reading the journal with Zoe that January afternoon, I realized that the letters in the ziplock bag are worth far more than beautiful objects.

. . . .

WORDS OF WISDOM FROM MOM, 1986

Throughout all of our joys and hard times I have found
that the secret ingredient to life is a positive outlook. At times
it has been difficult, but I have managed to hold my head up
high because of that strong determination to go for it.

I believe that I was meant to rediscover the letters now, in this season of my life. I have finally settled into who I am, and I am unapologetically me. At forty-eight, I've finally made peace with my mistakes, accepted the challenges that have come my way, shown myself an extra dose of grace. The rough edges of my personality have softened, and life experiences have given me a strong dose of compassion for others and myself. My heart is open to receiving all the good the Universe sends my way, and I'm committed to living my best life and being the best version of myself. Now I realize how helpful reading the letters years earlier would have been for me. My mom was incredibly positive and inspiring, and in her letters she was cheering me on. Reading her letters might have helped me gain the peace I spent so much time searching for, because her words would have reminded me to make the most of each day of my life. Instead of getting stuck in the pain and grief I often felt because I missed her so much, her words might have motivated me to stop feeling sorry for myself and get back to the business of living. But I can't go back. All I can do is move forward.

We can't control a lot of things in life, but we can wake up each day and decide to have a positive mindset. After her death, I forgot I had this power. I stopped approaching each day with determination to move forward and help myself feel happy. I stopped holding my head up high, and instead felt like a victim of life's circumstances, overcome with sadness and a longing that couldn't be fulfilled. I was angry at God and the unfair hand my family was dealt.

Believing good things will happen to you and maintaining a positive mindset isn't always easy. You have to be resilient when things don't go the way you want them to go, and remind yourself of your power. If you can learn to approach each day and each new opportunity with the determination to get the most out of your life, you will be more likely to get what you want and feel happier in the process.

"This one is strawberry flavored," my mom said. "This one is raspberry flavored. Now it's time for a chocolate one."

When I was a small child, my mom would tuck me into bed and kiss me many times all over my face. Each time she kissed me, she would tell me it was a different flavored kiss. All my favorite flavors, of course. I loved every kind of candy and couldn't get enough of this fun game. I would beg her for more kisses and flavors and it never got old. I didn't realize how special this experience was until I became a mom. When Zoe and Avi were little and I tucked them into bed, I played the same game with them. They would look at me with such big eyes, filled with delight, and couldn't wait to hear what flavor kiss I would plant onto their faces. Raspberry was the favorite. As I kissed my daughters, I thought about my mom, and it was sad to think that my daughters would never know her.

CHAPTER 2

The Circle of Life

During my senior year in college, I took a public speaking class and did a presentation titled "Dangers of the Sun." I dressed up like a lifeguard, blew a whistle at the beginning of the speech, and got an "A" on the presentation. My teacher had explained that it was important to catch the audience off guard, right from the beginning, and the whistle had done the job. I loved the class and felt like I was finally learning something I could use in the "real world." I was ready to be done with college and earn my own money.

"Public speaking is an important skill to have," my parents told me. "In business, it is beneficial to be able to speak well and communicate effectively." I worked hard on my speech, and tried to learn everything there was to know about skin cancer. I sent away for brochures and pamphlets, and studied pictures of the different kinds of skin cancer, including melanoma, the most dangerous form. I memorized statistics and charts, and since I was a finance major and good at numbers, I easily committed these figures to memory. I never knew that all that preparation would help me with more than that speech.

A couple of years later, on a trip with my family during one of the two weeks of vacation I got from my job in the "real world," I noticed my mom had a mole on the back of her shoulder that looked worrisome. The images of the different kinds of cancer immediately came to mind. While we were sightseeing and my mom was wearing a sleeveless shirt, I remember thinking to myself, *That doesn't look good.*

On the trip, I silently went through the ABCDEs of melanoma, something I had memorized for my speech:

Asymmetrical: Her freckle did have a strange shape to it.

Border: There was an uneven boarder to her freckle and it had many jagged edges.

Color: There were many different shades of brown through her freckle.

Diameter: Her freckle was larger than the size of a pencil eraser.

Evolving: It had changed because I had never noticed it before, and she usually wore sleeveless shirts when the weather was warm.

When I realized that the freckle on my mom's shoulder had all of these characteristics, a feeling of panic shot through me.

"Mom," I said while we were sightseeing and having a lot of fun, "the freckle on your shoulder really doesn't look good. You need to go to the doctor."

"You're worried about a little freckle?" she said, and laughed. "It's just a freckle. I'm fine."

"I think this could be serious," I said. "Promise me you will go see a doctor when we get home."

Months later, after I continued nagging her, she finally went to see a dermatologist. Back then, it wasn't very common to get your skin checked by a dermatologist. I had never been to one and didn't know many people who had, unless they had acne. It's not like it is now, when everyone has a doctor for everything and can call them on their cell phone by issuing an order to Siri. At the first appointment, the doctor immediately removed the freckle from my mom's shoulder, and sent it off to pathology.

A week later, we got the call we didn't want to get. It was melanoma.

Again, the statistics presented themselves in my mind. We waited while tests were ordered. Several nodes were removed from under her arm, and we braced ourselves for the results of the lymph node dissection that would determine her future. Our family's future. Had the melanoma spread to her lymph nodes or was it contained in just the one spot? Had we found it in time? Finally, we were told that her lymph nodes were clear and she would be fine. We celebrated our good fortune and thanked God that she would be okay. We didn't talk about what could have happened.

One night, my mom pulled me into her room, took off a beautiful blue sapphire and diamond ring she always wore, and as we sat on her bed, she tried to give it to me. "You saved my life," she said, "and I want you to have this."

"No," I said. "Are you kidding? I don't need your jewelry; I just need you. I don't know what I would do without you and I'm just so thankful you're okay." We held hands as we talked and hugged one another with tears in our eyes. We were blessed and didn't take it for granted. She was my person, my rock. The prior few weeks of waiting for the test results had been some of the hardest of my life. I had moved through them with anxiety, tears, and "what if" thoughts. Jon and I had only been married for a short time, and my parents were in the middle of building their dream home. They were living in a rental apartment, having sold the house we lived in when I was in high school as they looked forward to this new stage in their lives.

My mom saw her dermatologist every few months. If the doctor found a mole or freckle that looked suspicious, it would presumably be found early since she was being well monitored. Before her melanoma scare, my mom had loved sunbathing, sitting outside, and working on her tan. When I was growing up, I often came home from school and found my mom sitting outside in a lounge chair, reading a book. In her younger years, she often used baby oil, and did everything she could to enhance her "healthy glow." After this scare, she stopped her sun bathing, and we all tried to be careful. We always wore hats when we went outside and we applied sunblock.

Five years later, the same weekend I learned I was pregnant with Zoe, while visiting my parents in Virginia, I found out that my mom had stage four melanoma. The melanoma was now everywhere in her body. We weren't as lucky as we thought we were.

Apparently, some cells were left in her body from the original melanoma, and they had eventually "woken up," silently growing and spreading while she was busy living her life.

"How much time?" I heard my father ask the oncologist on the speaker phone in my parents' office. The doctor had ordered many different tests to gather a clear understanding of what we were dealing with, and my mom had been to several hospitals to get full body and brain scans. Her doctor was calling to explain the test results. He sounded sad, and I heard him say, "With really hard chemotherapy, probably around nine months." He paused and then added, "But you never know. Some people have done really well and have gone into remission. If anyone can do it, you can."

There was silence as my parents tried to digest this news.

"That will get you to the birth of your first grandchild," I heard my dad say to my mom in a voice I wasn't used to hearing. He sounded scared, and his voice shook as he talked. It broke my heart.

"I'm in for the fight of my life," my mom said to my dad and the doctor, "but I'm going to win."

She said this with such strength and determination, and I wanted to believe her. They didn't know I was eavesdropping on this conversation, but I couldn't pull myself away. As I sat on the floor outside their office, wearing my pink and white flannel pajamas and feeling panic flow through my body, I cried and wondered how this could be happening to my family. I wondered, *What did we do to deserve this? Why her? Why our family?*

My mom had always looked forward to being a grandmother and did not refrain from making little comments to Jon and me. "What are you waiting for," she would say. "I want a grandchild." Finally, we felt like the timing was right. But while I was thrilled to be pregnant, my heart ached for my mom.

As expected, the chemotherapy was hard. Each time my mom received it, every three weeks, she had to go to the hospital and stay there for a week. My parents didn't want me to visit my mom in the hospital. They wanted to protect me from seeing her so sick and didn't want to upset me, any more than I already was, while I was pregnant. I was happy to oblige. I was so emotionally distraught that I was afraid I would lose the baby. Then my mom would never get to see her grandchild.

It was difficult for my mom to check herself into the hospital, knowing she would experience horrible nausea and diarrhea. I was living in North Carolina and would sometimes call her when she was in the hospital. Often, she felt too sick to talk. Then I would cry because it was hard to think about her suffering. To help my mom and my family have something to look forward to, we planned a family cruise to Alaska later that summer, while I could still travel, and when she would be finished with chemo-therapy.

Jon and our parents and brothers did go on a cruise for a week, spending a few days on the front and back ends in different cities. My mom's most recent scans indicated that the chemotherapy was working, and we were all optimistic and hopeful. Though there was some cancer still in her body, it was still shrinking in some places and nothing had progressed. The trip was a beautiful opportunity for us to celebrate how well things were going. We laughed. We ate. We toured small villages in Alaska, walked through an iris field, and laughed some more. Mostly, we spent time talking and being together. We knew how special our time with one another was, and didn't take it for granted. I was five months pregnant and feeling fine.

"I wish we could stay on the ship forever," my mom said to me on the last night. We had packed our bags and put them outside our cabin doors to be taken off the ship in the morning, and it was hard to leave. "I feel safe on the ship," she said. "Like nothing bad can happen while we're here." We held hands and I had to fight back my tears. I knew if I started crying I might not be able to stop, and I didn't want her to see me that way. Here's a portion of a letter from my mom, sent to Jon and me via email, immediately after the trip:

I AM MY MOTHER'S DAUGHTER

*It is hard for Dad and me to accept that the "Big Trip"
has ended. Yet, the memories of laughter, sharing, and
experiencing will linger for a long time. It is always special to
spend time with our daughter and her husband, but to share
the excursion with Jon's family and to have had such a positive
experience is rare. The truth is that the success of the trip was
attributed to the respect we all had for each other. We understood
that we needed time alone as well as time with one another.
For Dad and I the group with all of you was supportive and
comforting as we focused on you and not ourselves. We love
that you have a commitment to family.*

As my belly got bigger and bigger, my mom got thinner and
weaker. There were times when we both felt sick, her from the chemotherapy, me from being pregnant, and we would sit and eat pop-
sicles together. Lime was my favorite, strawberry, hers. I tried to
spend as much time with her as I could, and since I didn't live in
Virginia, I visited her on the weekends. She spent several weekends
in the hospital, but she always seemed to bounce back after getting
fluids and steroids, and we convinced ourselves that she was just
dehydrated. We didn't talk about the possibility of her dying.

One evening, while visiting my parents in Virginia without Jon,
I started having what I assumed were contractions, and I begged my
dad to take me to the hospital.

"Something isn't right," I said.

It was a couple of weeks before my due date, and he didn't
really think I was having a baby. I called my doctor's office, but

the on-call doctor didn't seem concerned. I called Jon, but there wasn't much he could do. After a couple of hours, I went to the bathroom and saw blood in the toilet. We needed to go to the hospital. Since we couldn't leave my mom alone, we called my parents' best friends to come and stay with her. Aunt Bette was at home baking a cake to bring for dinner the next evening. She had to turn the oven off and leave the cake, but of course, was happy to do so. Since my dad had just bought a new car, he lined the whole front seat with trash bags so that I wouldn't mess it up if my water broke on the drive to the hospital. Finally, with me moaning in the front seat of the car, we got to the hospital.

"It turns out she is in labor," my dad said to Jon on the phone after a nurse checked to see if my cervix had dilated. "You better get on the road."

We were put into a room and I was given drugs to slow down the labor while we waited for Jon to drive from North Carolina to Virginia. We listened to relaxing music and dozed on and off.

"This feels strange," I said to my dad. "This place is a lot calmer than I thought it would be." We both smiled and laughed and fell asleep. My dad called my brother, who was in medical school in Richmond. A couple of hours later, the nurse came in and said it was time to start pushing; we couldn't wait anymore. And just as she said this, Jon showed up, as did my brother, and the three of them watched while I delivered Zoe. It was a little strange for my dad and brother to watch me have a baby, but at the time, I wasn't really thinking about that. An obstetrician I had never met delivered Zoe, and probably thought we were crazy to make my daughter's birth a family event.

My dad's generation wasn't allowed in the delivery room when their wives delivered babies, and he had never been with my mom when she delivered my brother or me. It was special for him to get to see a birth. We all needed some happiness, to be reminded of life and the beauty that comes from bringing new life into the world.

I had a lot of guests visit me in the hospital, especially since I was in Virginia, where I had grown up. Family and friends came to celebrate this joyful moment. But my mom hadn't come yet. I kept waiting for her to visit and for my dad to bring her to the hospital. I knew he was exhausted from being with me all night, but I longed to see my mom. Grandma Millie, my mom's mother, came and sat with me.

"Oh, Dara," she said, "your mom should be here. It should be her in this chair instead of me. I'm sorry for you but I will do my best to help you."

I didn't know what to say, and didn't want to admit what was happening. Late that afternoon, my dad brought my mom to see me and the baby. That's when I fully understood how sick my mom was. She wasn't able to walk into the hospital and had to use a wheelchair to get to my room. As I placed Zoe into her arms, and saw a look of joy and pride, I had to quickly put my hand underneath Zoe to support her and keep her from falling. That evening, when I was alone in the hospital room by myself, I couldn't sleep. I called the nurse and asked if she could call the doctor to give me something to help me sleep. I told her about my mom, what had happened that day, and we cried together.

The next day, before checking out of the hospital, as Jon and I were packing up, I started to feel anxious and panicky.

"I think something is wrong with me," I said to a new nurse. "I don't think I should leave."

"Let me check your vitals," she said.

After she determined that I was "fine," I realized what was wrong. I didn't want to go home and face what was happening to my mom.

I was having an anxiety attack. For nine months, the goal had been for my mom to live to see her first grandchild. Those were the words my dad had said that afternoon when her doctor gave her prognosis. Now that Zoe was here, and my mom had realized her goal, I was terrified of what was to come.

Several weeks later, at age fifty-two, my mom passed away.

I didn't know how to live in a world without my mom and, truthfully, I didn't want to. While it was a relief to not have to watch her suffer anymore, I felt lost and didn't know what to do. I was so used to asking her for advice and getting her opinion, or validation, regarding the decisions I was making. For the first time, I finally understood what it meant to have a broken heart. My heart physically hurt and I didn't know what to do about the pain.

I was used to talking to her each day around 5:00 p.m., even when she was sick, and all of a sudden, I didn't have anyone to talk to at this time. I was reminded daily of what had happened. Though I had amazing family and friends, they didn't understand what I was going through. Everyone kept saying, "We feel so sorry for you. You must be experiencing such opposite emotions. The joy of a baby and the sadness of losing your mom." This wasn't helpful, and my grief became overwhelming. I was one of the only people in my circle who had lost her mom.

Losing my mom a few weeks after I had my first daughter was one of the hardest challenges of my life. So many times I longed to talk with my mom, ask her questions, reminisce, and share with her things that only a mom would understand.

Ironically, my mom was an early childhood educator, the founder and director of a hugely successful nursery school, and a counselor of parents and young kids. I finally had a child I needed her expertise with, and she wasn't here to guide me. It was another reminder of how unfair life could be.

I tried to push all of my sadness away, tried to control everything I could control, and even distanced myself from my family. "I'm off the family," I told my brother. "I need a break." Since he was in medical school and was studying all the time, he didn't seem to notice. My dad was dealing with his own grief in his own way, going to temple every Friday evening and Saturday mornings and involving himself in temple activities. He also joined a support group for people who had lost a spouse, and encouraged me to join one as well for people who had lost a parent.

Eventually, Grandma Millie was diagnosed with breast cancer, and went through radiation. Once again, we called on the same doctor to help another member of my family. Her cancer was very slow growing and the doctor said she would be fine. I couldn't deal with more sickness, and for a few months, I walked away from it all. I rarely called or visited. I didn't want to get hurt ever again, and if pushing my loved ones away was what it took, I was game. It felt safer.

I settled into a clear understanding of what life was like without my mom. Instead of facing the pain head on, admitting I needed help and accepting what was going on, I distracted myself with everything I could come up with. I worked harder than I had ever worked, scheduled as many social events and activities as I could come up with, and did my best to push the sadness away. Jon was incredibly supportive. He understood how broken my heart was and did his best to cheer me up, but he couldn't bring my mom back.

We had a thriving social life, I poured myself into work, and Zoe was happy. I put a smile on my face and tried to convince myself that everything was great. But one can only pretend for so long.

· ·

WORDS OF WISDOM FROM MOM, 1992

There will be times when things are going astray.
What will help you through? Talking to yourself and saying,
"I can cope and make life work for me."
Remember this, Dara. It will assist you through
some hell that life throws to you.

These words were written to me in a card on my twenty-first birthday. Life was normal, and it was the summer before my senior year in college. Not everything had gone my way. I didn't love my summer job, and even though I was living with Jon in North Carolina so we could spend the summer together, I missed my family terribly. Jon was working at a law firm and his hours were terrible. I was spending a lot of time alone in a city where I didn't have any friends. As my mom often did, she was reminding me about the importance of staying positive.

My mom was a big fan of the words "I can cope." When she was initially diagnosed with stage four cancer, she even had a little handmade button with these words scribbled on it. You would think that this example of the power of our thoughts would have stayed with me. I wish I could say it had.

Truth be told, I had forgotten all of this, until I read the letters.

When she passed away, instead of helping myself by taking control of my thoughts and remembering how lucky I had been to have such an incredible mom, I made my life a lot harder. I focused on how much I missed her. I filled my mind with every negative thought you can imagine, felt sorry for myself and my family, and didn't even realize that I was doing this. I was angry at everyone, especially Jon. He was the lucky recipient of most of my anger, and after many months of arguing, we finally decided to go to a counselor. This was not only helpful for our marriage, it was helpful for me individually. While I had initially gone to a grief counselor, I hadn't understood what it meant to be "stuck in grief."

What I've come to realize, and what I wish I had known back then, is that the stories we tell ourselves become our reality, even if our perceptions aren't accurate. They're birthed by our fears, life events, the opinions of other people, what we've been taught, and our ego. My stories made me forget to count my blessings instead of my problems.

Awareness is key to changing this kind of pattern. You can't banish negative thoughts forever, but you can spend less time stuck in a negative space or fixated on scary "what if" scenarios. It may be uncomfortable, but if you lean into your emotions and face what you're feeling head on, you can figure out a way to help yourself. You can learn to recognize and replace negative stories and decide what you want to tell yourself and believe. You just have to pay attention to what you're thinking, and when you recognize you're saying something negative, you have to intentionally shift your negative thought to something positive.

As my mom said, when life gets hard and goes astray, ask yourself, "What can I do to make my life work for me?" or, "What will help me cope?"

For the most part, my family got along very well. That doesn't mean there weren't times when we argued with one another. There were also times when my mom argued with her mom and Grandma Margaret. Put a group of strong women or girls together, and over time, there's probably going to be a little arguing here and there.

There was one particularly bad argument I recall having with my mom, and I was reminded of this when I was reading the letters.

My mom had taken me to college orientation at the University of Alabama, along with my friend Allison, who would also be a freshman, and her mom. Instead of staying with Allison and going to the orientation event one evening, I went to a party with another girl I met who ended up being my first college roommate. I didn't tell my mom. I didn't call. I didn't tell Allison where we were going. I just went to a fun college party with my new friend. Several hours later, when I returned to the hotel, I found the following letter on the floor when I opened the door to the room. Allison was sleeping. (This letter was in the bag of letters.) On the outside of the letter was written, "Dara, please come to my room."

I AM MY MOTHER'S DAUGHTER

My Dear Dara,

*We have had an exciting four days at Alabama. You have
been excited about the roommate, the dorm, and many new
friendships. I have been very happy for you.*

*However, tonight disappointed me very much. You have not
considered how I feel about you being out so late. I am worried
about you. Have you been in an accident? Where are you? Never
have you been inconsiderate like this—NEVER.*

*I ask myself if this is what you will be like when your mother
and dad are not around. If so, you will burn out quickly. I am
hoping you will discuss this with me as I am very concerned,
hurt, and disappointed.*

Your Mother, with love

Needless to say, I felt horrible that night, but we talked about
it when I knocked on the door to my mom's hotel room. There we
were, in the hallway of the Sheraton Hotel, me with a slight buzz
from drinking a couple of beers and my mom in her nightgown,
trying to "discuss" what had happened without waking up Allison
or her mom. My mom was more upset with me that night than at
any other time I can remember. She was so shocked at my lack of
consideration for her feelings.

Now that I'm on the mom side of things, I know that I would
have been worried sick, and I totally understand how concerned
she was for my safety. Plus, she was probably dealing with a lot of

mixed emotions because I was about to leave home and go far away to school. Obviously, I didn't even consider this at the time. (It's not like I had a cell phone with an app she could use to track my every move, something Jon and I have done with our daughters for years.)

This letter reminds me that my relationship with my mom was real. It was honest. And it wasn't perfect. I'm glad I saved it. I wouldn't want to have only the "good" letters. I want to remember the full range of feelings expressed, even if some of the letters are hard to read.

CHAPTER 3

Wisdom from the Past

I sat on the couch in my family room at 10:16 p.m. on a Thursday night with the ziplock plastic bag on my lap. The bag was worn and old, and the contents inside the bag looked even older. There appeared to be well over one hundred cards and letters inside, most still in their original envelopes. I could see pink envelopes and striped ones, and what I imagined to be birthday and Valentine's Day cards. There were also plain white envelopes, some with folded up pieces of yellow legal paper inside. Each envelope was hand addressed to me, some with a camp address, including a cabin number, and others from my college years, with a University of Alabama address. I found it comforting to see the familiar handwritings. Though most of the people who wrote the letters had passed away, their words were still there, waiting for me.

For more than twenty or thirty years, depending on the letter, I put off rereading the letters. That evening, we had gone out to dinner with family and, while I rarely drink, I had enjoyed a glass of wine. It had been a fun evening, and when we got home, I wasn't tired. I was feeling calm and relaxed. Jon had gone to bed, Avi was locked in her room doing her homework, and Zoe was away at college. Sitting on the couch, thinking about the day, something told me to get the letters.

When I was little, I couldn't wait to get the mail to see if I had received something fun such as a *Highlights* magazine or an unexpected letter from a family member. I started attending summer camp when I was nine years old, for four weeks each summer, and eventually worked my way up to eight weeks. I loved getting mail even more at summer camp. In college, I couldn't wait to check my mailbox for a letter. It was always fun to get news from home, even though most of the time I quickly read the letter and then stuffed it back into the envelope and moved on with my day. While I appreciated what was written in the letters, it was the actual act of receiving the letters that I enjoyed the most, especially when I was younger.

"How many letters did you get?" someone in my cabin would ask.

"I got two today. How about you?" I always felt sorry for the kids who didn't receive any mail.

When I was younger, I didn't pay too much attention to what was being said in the letters. I was more concerned with the occasional stick of gum stuffed inside, or a fun sticker or a dollar bill someone sent to me to buy candy.

It was the early eighties, my first summer at camp, and I was nine years old. Those were the days before email, text messages, or even fax machines. The only way to communicate with people was via a telephone call or letter. Most of the time at camp, we weren't even allowed to make phone calls, which would have been expensive. Back then, letters were really the only form of communication when people were separated by distance. We didn't have social media pictures to stalk, email to send, or FaceTime to give us a glimpse of our loved ones.

While I was in college, cell phones had just hit the market and were very expensive. Most people I knew didn't have one. At first, my family decided I would call home each week on Sunday afternoon. My parents felt this would give me independence, but it was also cheaper to make long distance phone calls on Sundays. Because of this, I had a standing date with my family on Sunday afternoon. We would talk to one another for around twenty or thirty minutes. I usually cried when we hung up because I missed them so much. This plan lasted about a month, and then my mom and I started talking many times throughout the week, eventually working up to almost every day.

A couple years later, when I was a junior in college, Jon was in law school at the University of North Carolina. Now I had two separate long distance phone calls to make. To manage the expense, my dad had my long distance phone privileges cut off each month when the charges hit a hundred dollars, something that happened on a regular basis. After that, I had to call collect for the rest of the month, or wait until someone called me, hoping I was in my room to receive the call. Usually, when my phone hit the hundred dollar limit, there weren't many days left in the month. Because of this, letters still remained a great form of communication between me and the people I loved. I didn't know then that the letters would be a blessing.

Jon and I built our current home over twenty years ago. Eventually, all of my childhood belongings made it to this house. When my dad sold my parents' home and got remarried several years after the death of my mom, he brought me five boxes containing everything that had mattered to me most during my childhood. They were the first things I saw each morning when I got into my car to go to work, and they greeted me each day when I returned home. Yet I couldn't bring myself to open the boxes and look inside. They stayed in the garage, unopened, for almost five years.

My mom passed away in the month of November, and for a long time, I strongly disliked that time of year. In fact, in the early years after her death, I dreaded it. When the calendar changed from October to November, everything in my body tightened, and the memories of her death came flooding back. I was relieved when December 1 rolled around, and felt like a weight had been lifted off of my shoulders. "I made it," I would say to myself. "I don't have to deal with that for another year."

On the ten-year anniversary of her death, my heart felt especially heavy. *How could she have been gone for ten years?* I thought about all the events she had missed. Her death still seemed like a bad dream from which I hadn't yet woken up. At the time, my kids were little and home from school.

It was a lazy, cold November day, and out of the blue, Zoe mentioned the boxes. We were hanging out in the house, looking for something fun to do. "Why don't we go downstairs into the garage and open the boxes together?" she suggested in her perky little voice. "There might be things from Grandma Terri (the name I had taught my daughters to use when they talked about my mom) and she would want you to have them." I had previously told them about the contents in the boxes.

"Yes," said Avi, who usually agreed with Zoe. "Let's go do it right now." With two little girls looking at me with excitement, I was persuaded. On that November day, the three of us, each wearing our pajamas, went into the garage and opened the boxes. Having the girls with me made going through the boxes fun. They loved finding my childhood trinkets, books, old swimming medals, stuffed animals, baby dolls, and my favorite clothing. All of the items had sentimental meaning to me, but nothing was as important as the treasure I found buried in the last box: the ziplock bag. My kids weren't very excited about an old bag, and we didn't open it that day. I took the bag to the wooden dresser, where it stayed. I liked knowing it was safe in my house, even though I had never opened it.

As I sat on the couch that Thursday evening, with a cheering fire in the fireplace and a hot cup of tea, I knew I was as ready as I would ever be. I didn't know how reading the letters would make me feel. Would I be flooded with a longing that couldn't be satisfied? Was I opening myself up for pain I didn't need? I had worked so hard, gone through counseling and hospice support groups. I didn't want to bring it all up again, to reopen a wound that would take a long time to heal.

I sat there for a moment and took a deep breath. "I'm ready," I said out loud.

I pulled out the first note. It was from my mom, and I felt happy. I considered it a sign from her that I was doing the right thing. She would want me to read the letters, and I could handle whatever emotions got stirred up. As I read the letter, I was taken aback by how much her personality came through. It felt like I was having a conversation with her. I felt the tears starting, and I didn't try to hold them back. Like a kid grabbing candy, I grabbed another letter. I sat there reading the letters well into the night. When I was done, I let myself have a good cry. The ugly cry. The one that Oprah always talks about. I remembered the happy times in my childhood, the harder times when we lost a family member, and everything in between. It was all there, written in everyday words, by the people who had loved and raised me. I missed them. Longed for them. Cried for them.

At the same time, reading the letters I felt as if I was having an adult conversation with the people who had written them. These letters let me see what their lives were like through my adult eyes. While I thought I knew them well, and even though we'd spent a lot of time together, I'd seen them through the eyes of a child, pre-teen, teen, and young adult. I didn't completely understand their struggles, challenges, joys, or what brought them peace and happiness. How could I? I was just a kid, more concerned with my life and what was going on in my world.

I realized, from my forty-seven-year-old adult perspective, how treasured and adored I was, and how blessed I was to have been loved and nurtured by these people. I had assumed that, since the letters had been written to me as a young person, they wouldn't contain any thoughts that would be relevant to me as an adult. I was so very wrong. The wisdom that was inside each envelope applied to my life today.

I finally went to bed that night, but could hardly sleep. I wanted to wake up Jon and tell him what I had experienced. I felt like I had just had a coffee date—the kind that lasts three hours and is filled with beautiful, meaningful conversation with people who get you and care about you unconditionally. I always knew that I had had a happy childhood. But it wasn't until that evening on the couch that I fully understood how special I was to the people who raised me. I was their girl, and they wanted only good things for me. They walked beside me, through my life, feeling my successes and failures, cheering me on, guiding and advising me, every step of the way. My wins were their wins. My challenges were their challenges.

. . . .

LETTER FROM MOM, 1982

Dearest Dara,

This week we will be picking you up! We miss you very very much. On one hand we realize that our family is not complete without you. On the other hand we realize that our family bond is very close and that we are together in thoughts even when we are miles apart. We thought of you often, hoping you were healthy and happy. But, your Dad and I have learned we can let you out of our sight and still feel close to you. You see Dara, love is a bond that cannot be broken and love is letting you and Ari become independent. Of course you have parents and grandparents to help you along. But what you are learning is to stand on your own two feet. I think that when we are all together we will appreciate each other. Without a doubt we are a special family. Now, please make the most of camp.

Love, Mom

. . . .

It's strange how a random Thursday evening, on a dark and cold January night, completely shifted my thoughts, changed my perspective, and helped redefine the way I viewed my life and my losses. Opening the bag of letters that night helped me to release the pain I'd been holding onto for almost twenty years. The worn bag I had tried so hard to ignore was actually a way out of the grief I had gotten used to living with for most of my adult life.

. . . .

WORDS OF WISDOM FROM MOM, 1990

Life has a way of working out. Life has a way
of giving us the strength to meet the challenges
before us. No one can predict what will be. The key is
taking each day as it comes and making it work for you.
Allow life's magic to unfold.

What I've learned from everything I've been through is that life really does have a way of working out. This doesn't mean everything is going to always go the way you want it to go or that life isn't hard. What it does mean is that whatever you're facing and dealing with, things will more than likely work out. Maybe not right away, or the way you envisioned, but over time things tend to sort themselves out. It's called keeping your perspective, and it can really help you when you find yourself worrying about something or feeling like you aren't strong enough to get through whatever it is that life tosses your way. Life is uncertain for all of us. We don't know what will happen and it can be anxiety provoking to realize this. If we really thought about all the bad things that could happen to us in a given day, we probably wouldn't leave our homes. But this mindset wouldn't allow us to live each day to the fullest. As my mom said above, trust that life will work out, and that you do have the strength to get through whatever it is you're dealing with. Even though I lost my mom way too early, as hard as it's been, things have worked out. Somehow, I was able to find the strength to meet the challenges I was forced to face.

If you let yourself relax a little bit, and let go of trying to control every outcome of every situation, you will feel lighter and calmer. You will also probably find yourself enjoying whatever it is you're doing. By letting go and trusting, and having faith that good things will happen to you, you will allow life's magic to unfold. And here's the really amazing part: life can be so much better than we could ever imagine. I couldn't have predicted Zoe would discover her journal that January afternoon, or that reading it would lead me to finally open the ziplock bag after all these years. When I think about the magic this beautiful experience has brought to me, the peace and joy I've had because of it, I realize how right my mom was. Take one day at a time, try to live in the present moment, and trust that everything will work out. As I find myself telling my daughters regularly, "Expect good things to happen. They usually do."

One Halloween, Avi decided she wanted to go out with her friends to a party that evening. It was a Thursday, and even though she didn't have school the following day, she was going out of town for the next four days and wasn't going to get much sleep. Jon and I told her she could stay out until 10:30 p.m., but being the teenager she was, this wasn't good enough for her. She wanted more.

All day long, she sent Jon and me text messages, telling us we were being unreasonable, asking us to reconsider, begging us to let her stay out later. "Why are you treating me like a baby?" she kept asking, via text message. "You're being so unreasonable. Why don't you trust me? I'm such a good kid!" For the most part, I ignored these texts.

When Avi got home from school, she started up again.

"I'm not discussing this with you," I told her. "We aren't going to change our minds. You aren't being punished; we just want you to get a good night's sleep. You're about to be really busy and have a ton of fun and we want you to start out rested."

She refused to understand. I left the kitchen, where I was when she came home from school, and headed to my office. I needed space.

This time, I was the mom, raising a teenage daughter, and trying to balance my desire to maintain our beautiful relationship while setting necessary boundaries for Avi. It isn't easy being on the parent side of things, but I reminded myself of how nothing is perfect, and I'm doing the best I can. As I had this internal dialogue, my cell phone rang and it was Zoe, calling from college. "Hi," I said. "How are you?" We talked for a moment, and I could almost predict what was coming. "So," she said, "Avi asked me to call you. If you want my opinion, I think 10:30 p.m. is too early." I laughed, enjoying this, and then said, "Please don't. We aren't having this conversation." She laughed too, and then we moved on. Truth be told, I love that my daughters are close, even if what sometimes brings them together is their frustration with me. Zoe and I hung up the phone and I couldn't help but wonder, as I often do, "What would my mom say about all of this?" About my two daughters, about my parenting skills, about how things are going over here. I had a feeling that I knew, and a smile formed across my face. Life is magical, even with the frustration and teenage tears, and I count my blessings because, underneath all the normal daily living, the chaos of everyday life, there's so much love here, between all of us, and we are very lucky.

CHAPTER 4

If I Found One Journal, Surely I Could Find Another

A few days later, on another cold January evening, with my mind still spinning from the letters I had read and all the love I was feeling, a brilliant thought crossed my mind. Since we found Zoe's journal in my room, surely the probability of Avi's being there was pretty high.

I washed off the cleanser I was using and grabbed my eyeglasses. Then I hurried into my room and started opening up every drawer I could get my hands on. If Jon had come into the room at that moment, I'm sure he would have asked himself, *What is my crazy wife up to now?* But he didn't come in and I didn't have to explain myself. I have a "normal" routine that I follow to relax and release the day and to help me get into calm sleep mode. It includes a hot bath with essential oils and Epsom salts, usually followed by writing in my journal and a short meditation. But in that moment, all the relaxation I had generated from my bath was gone, and a good night's sleep wasn't likely.

In the drawers I found old sunglasses, books I hadn't read yet, pens, pencils, hair bands, and many other things I hadn't looked at in years. Underneath all the mess and clutter was Avi's mommy-daughter journal. I felt as happy as I did when Zoe's journal was discovered, and I couldn't wait to dig in and see what it said. I wanted to remember the little girl who would only wear dresses and pink clothes, who laughed hard and often, and played with her baby dolls for hours every day. Here is Avi's first entry to me:

MOMMY-DAUGHTER JOURNAL ENTRY, 2011

Dear Mommy,

I love you so much and I hope you are having a wonderful day. And this is what you are to me: awesome, gr8, wonderful, best, loving, best mommy in the world, happy, cool, nice, hugging, kissing. Once upon a time there was a best mommy in the world and there was an Avi and they were best friends. And they told each other everything and that made Avi happy. The end.
I love you!!!

Love, Avi

Reading this, I had tears in my eyes. I could see in my mind's eye the little girl who wrote this: my adorable "Avi Girl," as I used to call her. She is dressed in a pink smocked dress, wearing a matching bow in her hair, and she thinks I am the most amazing person in the world. Avi is now seventeen. We have been in the throes of the teenage years, and it hasn't always been easy between us, especially since Zoe went away to college. Avi does not like the role of only child. She misses Zoe terribly and feels that Jon and I are too focused on her. She texts me pictures of helicopters spinning as a way of telling me that I am being too overprotective and making her follow too many rules. Of course, she forgets that Zoe lived by those same rules, just as I sometimes forget that Zoe and I had these same kinds of issues when she was living at home.

Avi has been pushing boundaries. Recently, for the first time, she became distant with me. It was like there was an invisible line that she wouldn't let me cross, and it was heart-wrenching. I longed for us to be close and to really talk, not about homework assignments or what her plans were, but about things that really mattered. Sadly, in this season of our relationship, nothing I tried seemed to work. I took her to her counselor to help figure out what was going on with her, to try to help her, but it didn't feel like we were moving forward. When I brought this up with Jon, he reminded me, "Dara, this is just a stage; she'll grow out of it. We went through this with Zoe." While I knew he was right, I wanted to fix it. What I've learned is that some things can't be fixed, especially on our timetable. They have to work themselves out, and I have to be patient.

My heart felt a little heavy as I read her words, written at a simpler time in our lives. Then I thought of all the stages we've been through together, and told myself we would get through this one as well. I vowed to start writing to her again; maybe this would be a good way for us to communicate about meaningful things. I was tired of just talking about her daily plans, reminding her to take her stuff to her room, or arguing about why she couldn't do what she thought she should be allowed to do. I wanted to hear about her feelings, what she was really going through, the challenges and stresses she was experiencing. Maybe, this was the Universe, sending me the tool we needed to get back on track.

I stopped reading the journal, walked to my desk in our sunroom, and found a notebook that was in pretty good shape. Then I wrote a note to Avi, from my heart to hers. I told her how much I loved her, how proud of her I was, and how blessed I felt to have her as my daughter. I was always telling her these things, but I wasn't sure she was always listening to me. Reading these words might not change things between us immediately, but it was a good start. I planned to put the notebook on her pillow in the morning, after she left for school, just as we had done long ago. When I got into bed that night and continued reading Avi's mommy-daughter journal, I was feeling optimistic. Here is one of my early entries to Avi:

MOMMY-DAUGHTER JOURNAL ENTRY, 2011

Dear Avi,

It has been such a fun morning with you! You tried on 1,000 dresses and bows. We always have so much fun together. You are such a joy and I am so lucky to get to be your mommy. Thank you for always being a ray of sunshine in my life. I love you. I love you. I love you! I hope you have a fun night tonight at the dance recital. Enjoy every moment of your life!

Love, Mommy

This is another entry from Avi, one of my favorites because it's so childlike and innocent:

· ·

MOMMY-DAUGHTER JOURNAL ENTRY, 2011

Dear Mommy,

You are the best mommy girl in the world!! I love you more than pancakes. I love you more than sugar. I love you more than pigs. I love you more than baby dolls. I love you more than my room. I hope you get it now. I am having so much fun with you.

Love, Avi
· · · · · · ·

Sadly, just like Zoe's journal, Avi's journal suddenly stopped. I knew why. Sure, as the girls got older and life became busier, there wasn't as much time for writing. But that wasn't the only reason. The real reason, the one that changed our lives, was something that had come out of nowhere and thrown me off my game. When I was forty-two years old, in the middle of raising my family and living my life, I had been diagnosed with cancer.

· · · · · · · · · · · · · · · · · · · ·

WORDS OF WISDOM
FROM GRANDMA MARGARET, 1981

Try to enjoy every day.

Such simple, never-outdated advice can have a profound impact on our lives. It's easy to get so caught up in thinking about what isn't working, what we "must" or "should" do, or worrying about the things in our lives we can't change, that we forget to concentrate on the now, the day we're actually living. When little Avi wrote those entries, she wasn't thinking about the stresses of life, or consumed with the past or future. She was just happy to be in the moment, playing with dolls, trying on dresses, enjoying her day.

Grandma Margaret knew about this. She had been through unimaginable pain and sorrow. My dad's parents, Grandma Margaret and Grandpa Kurt, who was a surgeon, fled Nazi Germany and came to this country with few possessions and little money. They eventually settled in the small town of Franklin, Virginia. My grandmother was pregnant with my uncle Jack when she entered Ellis Island, a secret they couldn't share with anyone since she wouldn't have been able to enter the country pregnant. Once here, they raised two sons, Jack and my father, Harry, and worked hard to become American, involving themselves in the community while doing their best to make peace with their past. They eventually learned that their parents and grandparents had all been killed in concentration camps. I knew they had been through a lot, but they never talked about these things. They were devoted to their family, had a strong commitment to their Jewish identity, and felt education was extremely important. I knew they carried a lot of sadness and guilt because of the Holocaust, but they focused on living in the moment.

I AM MY MOTHER'S DAUGHTER

LETTER FROM GRANDMA MARGARET, 1986

Dear Dara,

Today is the 4th of July. I hope you are celebrating a little at camp. I watched T.V. It is such a beautiful sight to see these big tall sailboats from all over the world passing by "Miss Liberty." I remember when grandpa and I got our first glimpse of the Statue of Liberty. We were all standing on the decks of the "Britannica," a big ship crossing the Atlantic Ocean. We were very happy to see this welcoming statue. We arrived on grandpa's birthday, June 21, 1940.

How are you? Are you keeping very busy? Do you need anything? I hope you are having a very good time. Keep well and take good care. I love you,

Grandma

My grandparents corresponded with their family members who had been able to get out of Germany and who eventually moved to Israel, and when I was in high school, we took a family trip to Israel for the first time to meet our huge family there. Since then, I've been to Israel many times, and have managed to keep in touch with several family members there. Right before Zoe's Bat Mitzvah, we took a trip to Israel to introduce our kids to them.

A couple of years ago, Jon and I took Zoe and Avi to Berlin, where Margaret grew up. She used to share stories of her childhood before the war with me. As I gazed at the site where her building once stood, my connection to her deepened. I closed my eyes and, with the sun shining on my face, thought about her happy childhood and how she had to leave Germany. She had been incredibly strong and coped with the unimaginable. Then she moved forward, making life work for her and her family.

I know we won't enjoy every moment of our lives. However, if we can remind ourselves to look for enjoyment, we can help ourselves. I believe every person has the right to be happy. Not all the time, and not every day. But, hopefully, most days. If we can intentionally carve out moments of joy each day, we can go to sleep at night confident that we made the day work for us, even in life's more challenging seasons. It's an attitude, a choice, and we each get to make it for ourselves.

As I was realizing, reading the letters and the journal entries, our lives are made up of moments. Sure, there are the big moments in life: weddings, the birth of a child, a new house, a job promotion. But it's important to appreciate the simple pleasures, the "normal" moments that we experience most of the time in our daily lives. After all, this is where we tend to spend most of our time.

Both of my grandmothers loved cooking. When my mom passed away, my mom's sister, Shelli, and her daughter, Bonni, along with Grandma Millie, would come once a year to North Carolina to visit my family. We would hang out, talk about anything and everything, laugh a lot, and cook. Grandma Millie loved teaching us her special recipes, even though most of the time she didn't use exact measurements. She would use a little of this and a little of that. I tried to get her to go slowly, frantically writing the directions down, so we would be able to replicate her delicious dishes. My favorite of all her recipes was her potato casserole, which is very easy to make, and tastes like you spent all day in the kitchen.

Grandma Millie's kitchen was very small, and it always amazed me to think about the quantity of food she prepared in such a small space. She had one oven, limited counter space, a small breakfast table, and a stacked washing machine and dryer. Her dining room table was always set with a tablecloth, napkins, and mixed dishes, depending on how many people were there. The room was often packed with people, and she would bring out each dish, one at a time, and place it on the dining room table with pride. She loved cooking for people, and no one was ever turned away. If you wanted to eat dinner with her and you didn't mind sitting around a crowded table, you would be invited. I think of this often when I'm cooking in my huge kitchen with my double ovens. After she passed away and my aunt went through Millie's things, I was fortunate enough to inherit two of her casserole dishes. I use these weekly, and always think about her when I pull one of these out of the cabinet. I know she would love the idea of my cooking with her precious bakeware. Though she used a box of instant potatoes, you can make this by boiling six large fresh-peeled potatoes, a healthier choice. This is how I tend to make it now.

. . . .

Grandma Millie's Potato Casserole

INGREDIENTS

4 big Vidalia onions
olive oil
1 cup hot water
1 box instant potatoes
¾ cup skim milk
2 eggs
1 small container sour cream
garlic power
salt
pepper

DIRECTIONS

Chop the onions and sauté in olive oil. Pour olive oil onto the bottom of your large casserole dish or metal pan. Pour the box of instant potatoes (or the mashed fresh potatoes) into the casserole dish and add one cup of hot water. Mix with your hands, and add more water if necessary. You don't want it to be too thick or runny. Take half of the onions and spread them over the potato mixture. Add the milk, sour cream, and eggs, and sprinkle with salt, pepper, and garlic powder. Mix everything together, then use a knife to make the top flat, and sprinkle with olive oil. Add the rest of the onions, pushing them into the potatoes. Cook, uncovered, for one hour or until the top is browned. It will rise and make your house smell amazing.

Grandma Margaret loved to cook also, but coming from Germany, she had a completely different cooking style. She preferred to cook her meals on top of the stove, and especially loved to bake American dishes. She was always cutting out recipes from *Good Housekeeping* magazine and trying new desserts. Whenever we had family time, be it going to the beach, a park, or even an evening concert, she would always pack a cooler and bring sandwiches and dessert. She made different kinds of sandwiches, trying lots of different combinations. Once, she took peanut butter crackers and put them between slices of bread to make peanut butter cracker sandwiches! (This didn't go over very well.) My favorite was a meatloaf sandwich made on rye bread with ketchup and sweet pickles. It doesn't sound very good, but it was fabulous. Grandma Margaret wrapped everything perfectly in wax paper and labeled things neatly. I don't think she had any "junk drawers" in any of her homes. She always packed a homemade sweet treat for us, and her carrot cake was my favorite.

I couldn't help but share the next recipe because it is my favorite recipe from this grandmother. I've made it for my daughters many times and they love it. She always made it as a Bundt cake and brought along an extra container of the cream cheese frosting because we all loved it so much and wanted more. It isn't the healthiest dessert but it's the best.

. . . .

Grandma Margaret's Carrot Cake

INGREDIENTS

2 ½ cups sifted flour

2 cups sugar

2 teaspoons baking powder

1 ½ teaspoons baking soda

2 teaspoons cinnamon

4 eggs

1 ½ cups cooking oil

2 cups grated carrots

1 cup crushed pineapple with syrup

2 teaspoons vanilla

CREAM CHEESE FROSTING

1 (3 ounce) package cream cheese

1 teaspoon vanilla

1 ½ cups confectioners' sugar

DIRECTIONS

In a large bowl, stir together the dry ingredients.
Add the oil, eggs, carrots, pineapple, and vanilla. Mix until
all ingredients are moistened. Beat with an electric mixer
for two minutes at medium speed. Pour the batter into a
greased and lightly floured 9 x 13-inch baking ban. Bake at
350 degrees for sixty minutes. Cool. Frost with the cream
cheese frosting. Blend the cream cheese and vanilla, slowly
add confectioners' sugar, and beat until smooth. Spread
over the cake and let the frosting drip down the sides.

When I got married, the theme of one of my bridal showers was a Kitchen Shower. Everyone was instructed to bring a recipe. Here's the recipe my mom brought to that shower over twenty-five years ago. When I make this now, I use organic dairy products, always.

. . . .
Mom's Manicotti

INGREDIENTS

1 box manicotti noodles

olive oil

1 container nonfat cottage cheese

1 jar spaghetti sauce

1 package mushrooms, chopped

½ onion, chopped

1 package mozzarella cheese

1 package Parmesan cheese

½ teaspoon dried oregano

½ teaspoon dried parsley

salt and pepper

DIRECTIONS

Boil the noodles in a large pot with a little oil and, once done, let the noodles cool. While the noodles are boiling, cook the chopped onion and mushrooms in a little olive oil until fully cooked. In a separate bowl, mix together the cottage cheese, Parmesan cheese, herbs, and a dash of salt and pepper. Mix in the cooked onion and mushrooms. Spray a baking dish with a little oil. Once the noodles cool, rinse each noodle, make a slit on one side, and spoon in the mixture. After all the noodles are done, pour the sauce over them. Bake, covered, at 350 degrees until the sauce bubbles. Keep covered until you are ready to serve and then place the mozzarella cheese on top. Bake for another ten minutes, uncovered. Serve with salad, bread, fruit and sauteed zucchini.

Here is my kids' favorite recipe that I make, and we tend to have it a lot because I can count on everyone eating dinner that night. It's super easy, and you can make it ahead of time or even freeze it. Walnuts are a healthy alternative to pine nuts, usually used for making pesto, and you can't tell the difference.

. . . .
Dara's Pesto

INGREDIENTS
> 1 cup packed fresh basil.
> 2 large garlic cloves
> ¾ cup olive oil
> ½ cup walnuts
> ¾ cup organic Parmesan cheese
> salt and pepper to taste

DIRECTIONS
> In a Vitamix or food processor, mix the basil, garlic, olive oil, walnuts, and cheese together until completely combined into a sauce. Add the salt and pepper to taste. Serve on top of whole wheat noodles with a side of broccoli and a salad. You can serve it with organic sliced chicken if you would like.

CHAPTER 5

Life Got Messy

I was forty-two when I heard the terrifying words, "You have cancer," and the girls were eleven and fourteen. One day life was great, and then the next, out of nowhere, I was hearing words like mass, chemotherapy, surgery. These aren't the words anyone wants to hear, but being a mom of two young daughters, this news was terrifying. I knew how hard it was to live in a world without my mom, and I didn't want this to happen to my daughters. The diagnosis hit me harder than I could have imagined. It put me smack back into memories of when my mom was sick.

There were so many lessons I hadn't yet taught my daughters. There were things I wanted us to do together, big life moments I wanted to share with them. The nightmare was happening again—only this time, I was the mom. Cancer seemed to continue down the lineage of my family, and this time it was my turn. While I had a favorable diagnosis, it was still cancer, and I remembered that my mom was also expected to be fine. Then, five years later, she wasn't. I couldn't stop thinking about cancer. If something like that could happen to her, I knew it could happen to me. I wanted to trust that I would be okay, but it wasn't easy. My ability to trust had been buried along with my mom.

"You thought you were going to die," my dad said to me, several years later as we were sitting on the couch in my den. He said, "For a long time you didn't trust that you would make it, even though we tried to tell you there was every reason to believe you would." My dad cleared his throat, as he does when we're talking about something heavy. I shrugged when I heard this and squeezed his hand. Our relationship has grown significantly over the past years. We were always close, but when my mom was living she took center stage in my life. When she passed away, my dad and I leaned into one another.

When I was on the table, having the biopsy done to see if what looked like cancer in the ultrasound was actually cancer, the doctor told me that I needed to prepare myself. I listened as he described what that meant, and I sobbed. I told him what had happened to my mom and how devastating it had been for my family. I sobbed some more. He patiently listened, as he extracted what was needed for the biopsy. I could see the sadness in his eyes. He understood that there were no guarantees.

Several days later, Jon and I finally met with the nurse navigator to get all of the results, go over the pathology, and find out what we were actually dealing with. That's when the nurse navigator turned to me and said, "Dara, this isn't your mom's story. This is your story. Her ending isn't going to be your ending." There were no better words she could have said to me. I had to keep repeating them, over and over again, as I went through surgery, chemotherapy, radiation, and more surgery. But it wasn't until several years later, after I had been through a lot of counseling and committed myself to letting go of all the fear that followed me around like my shadow, that I fully understand the impact my mom's illness had on my own. While I was in treatment, I felt guilty to have the prognosis I had, while she had been dealt such a cruel hand.

Jon and I waited until we had the full picture of my diagnosis and treatment plan before telling the girls about my diagnosis. I wanted to be as aggressive as possible, and it was decided that I would have a double mastectomy with reconstruction, wait a couple of weeks, and then start chemotherapy. I would do eight rounds of chemotherapy and then do radiation. After this, I would have another surgery to replace the expanders with my real implants and then have a hysterectomy. All of this would take a year, and it felt impossible. I would also do genetic testing to see if there was a connection to my mom's cancer and Grandma Millie's breast cancer. Her daughter, Shelli, had also had breast cancer.

I'll never forget the sound of Avi hyperventilating when we told her I had breast cancer. One minute, her life was great, and then, on a Friday afternoon after school when she was having a snack, her world came crashing down on her. Both my daughters were distraught, and clung to one another. They started sleeping with each other, and even though we told them I would be fine, I'm not sure they believed it. I wasn't sure myself. I was barely keeping it together, and at times I felt like I was drowning. I tried to be strong for my daughters and put on a good front, but one can only pretend for so long.

Sensing that I was close to the edge, my dad and stepmother came to stay with my family every other week during the four months I went through chemotherapy. This gesture of love was exactly what we needed. I had always been close to my dad and stepmother, but our relationship grew even more during this time. My in-laws also pitched in, and getting me better while making sure the kids maintained some form of normalcy became a family priority. They say it takes a village. For us, it took the love of our family and friends to pull us through.

When my hair began to fall out, my daughters fully registered what was going on. Before then, most of my treatments had occurred when they were at school, and I didn't look sick. Seeing me this way was disturbing for them, and I felt responsible for their unhappiness.

I felt guilty for being diagnosed.

I felt guilty for putting them through this experience.

I felt guilty for having a significantly better prognosis than my mom.

I remembered when she lost her hair. I relived her experience. As much as I wanted to focus on taking care of myself and my daughters, I kept thinking about what my mom had gone through, and how hard it must have been for her. I would turn to Jon, crying, wondering how my mom had faced her ordeal with such strength. She had felt, from day one, that she was going to beat her sentence. As a result, we all believed it. "How did she do it?" I would say to Jon. "She must have been so scared." My mom never shared any of her fears with me, and we never talked about what could happen. We never discussed anything but her beating the cancer and getting better. I was her pregnant daughter, and I'm sure she was trying to protect me.

"Did Mom talk to you about dying?" I asked my dad one day. "Of course," he said, taking a deep breath. "But once we made the commitment to the treatment plan, we played to win. You can't go through something like that unless you expect to get the outcome you want." This made a lot of sense to me. I was playing to win my own battle.

I got through my treatment plan, my hair started to grow back, and life began to feel more normal. The doctors said that everything looked great, and that it was "time for you to go back to living your life." Nothing showed up on any of the genetic tests, a huge relief for Zoe and Avi. Yet, mentally, I was a mess. I didn't know it then, but I had a lot of work to do—years of pain and grief to deal with and peace to find. I had to learn not only to say, "My story wasn't my mom's story," but I had to really believe it. I needed the courage to accept what had happened to her and to me, make peace with my diagnosis, and give myself permission to move forward with my life, even though she wasn't able to move forward with hers. Jewish guilt is real, and I had more than my share of it.

I've tried to explain Jewish guilt to my non-Jewish friends. While it's often a source of humor and jest—as in portrayals of a nagging "Jewish mom" who makes her kids feel badly about not doing something she wants them to do—there isn't really anything funny about it. Truthfully, I believe the Holocaust played a role in the development of Jewish guilt, because survivors of the Holocaust often felt terribly guilty about living while so many of their loved ones had passed away. I saw this firsthand. It wasn't until I was an adult that I could put a name to it: "survivors' guilt." This Jewish guilt runs deeply through my family, and has been passed on from one generation to the next. We're all so connected, one generation to the next, in positive and not so positive ways.

. . . .
LETTER FROM GRANDMA MARGARET, 1988

My Dear Dara,

Today came your nice letter. I can't tell you how happy I am to hear that you are having a good time and that being in Israel is meaningful to you. Being there is really special and one has to stop once in a while and think. I'm sorry I can't be at the airport when you arrive home. I do not like to say "good-by" very much but I love to say "hello!" Well my dear, enjoy the rest of your stay in the land of our forefathers. Make the most of it and take good care of my granddaughter. I love you,

Grandma
. . . .

While I never discussed with Grandma Margaret or Grandpa Kurt what they went through, and how their hearts must have been broken beyond belief, I know my dad grew up in a serious home that emphasized education, making the world better, and committing to Judaism. They focused on building their life in America and didn't want to talk about their past. It was too painful. It always amazed me to see how devoted my grandparents were to God. They never seemed angry at God for what had happened to them and their family. I couldn't say the same. I was pretty angry at God for taking my mom away from me.

When my mom was really sick and things weren't looking good, I started bargaining with God. "Hey, God," I would say. "If I do X, how about you let her test go well," or, "If I do Y, please help Mom get a good scan result. If I promise to do Z, will you make sure she lives?" I came up with all sorts of things I would be willing to do if God would just meet me halfway. My negotiating skills were becoming fine-tuned. Then my mom passed away. To say I was pissed off at God is an understatement. "I thought we had a deal!" I remember saying to God. "So much for you doing your part." And, just like that, I was done with having faith and talking to God.

I watched my dad strengthen his relationship with God, praying almost every morning, going to temple every weekend, and doing a lot of reading and learning. But I was over it. I still celebrated all the holidays, and when my kids were old enough, they started attending Sunday school and then Hebrew school, but as for my personal spiritual practice, I didn't have one. I was a cultural Jew, could make a really good kugel, and liked eating a bagel with lox and cream cheese just as much as any other "good" Jewish girl. God had let me down when I really needed some help, and I was never going to forget it.

When I was diagnosed with cancer, people would say to me, "I'll pray for you, Dara," or, "I've added you to my church's prayer list." They said this with such love and devotion, and while I really appreciated it, I wasn't convinced it would do any good. Part of me wanted to tell them, "That's nice, but I'm not sure there's anyone listening to you." Reaching out to God while I was trying to get through my treatments wasn't something I wanted to do. There were times when I felt a little guilty about this. If everyone was praying for me, the least I could do was pray for myself. But even in those dark moments, when I tried to reach out to God, I just couldn't do it.

When I was finally done with treatment, things got really challenging for me. I didn't know what to do or where to turn. I had been focused on getting through my treatment for so long that, although I was grateful to be done, it brought on a slew of emotions that I wasn't prepared for. I felt lost, scared, and depressed. I knew I didn't want to live the rest of my life this way and was willing to try anything to help myself feel better.

That's when I developed my spiritual practice and realized that I do believe in the power of the Universe, and I know with certainty that the Universe wants good things to come my way. This spiritual awakening didn't happen overnight. I struggled. I talked to anyone who was willing to talk to me, and read everything I could get my hands on. I struggled some more. I felt deep pain and anxiety, pushed through it, learned more, and figured out what worked for me, what made sense to me, and what I could trust.

I'm not here to tell you what to believe in. Whether you believe in Jesus, Allah, Buddha, God, or the Universe is your personal business. What I will say is that having faith and trusting in something will probably help you navigate the waters of your life and the challenges everyone eventually faces. Being able to lean on something that feels right to you when you don't know where to turn, or when things don't work out the way you want them to, is a beautiful gift you can give yourself. I know the spiritual practice I have today would have really helped me when I was going through the challenging times of my past. I don't regret not having it, though, because it just wasn't my time. I had to go through what I did to be where I am today, and I hope you can learn from me.

If you want to have a spiritual relationship with a higher power, you've got to do the work. Explore whatever feels right to you in a judgment-free zone. Read. Talk to your rabbi or minister. Seek out friends and family members who find strength in their faith, whatever it may be, and ask them questions. If you're feeling guilty about your current relationship with a higher power, give yourself a pass. If you feel you let your parents down because you don't believe the way you were brought up to believe, or you're afraid you aren't a good Jew or a good Christian or a good follower of whatever religion you subscribe to, let these feelings go. You haven't messed up, and it's never too late. Regardless of what you believe in or don't believe in, bringing a spiritual practice into your life is a beautiful way for you to learn to calm your mind, manage stress, and connect to your highest self. You can't live a truly authentic life if you don't take the time to listen to the little voice inside you, the one most of us shut down throughout our lives. I didn't fully understand this until I stumbled into a spiritual practice during my quest to learn, but it's been a game changer for me.

During all of this, the last thing I was thinking about was writing to my daughters in their mommy-daughter journals, and they weren't writing to me either. We were each struggling with our own fears, going to individual counseling sessions, and trying to make sense of what had happened. We weren't able to open up and share our thoughts and feelings about the experience or the fear of something happening to me. We were each trying to be strong for the other, and none of us was ready to face our fears. We each sensed that we were only as strong as our weakest link. If one of us buckled, the other might break.

Looking back, it's easy for me to think that writing in the journals might have helped my daughters work through some of their anxiety and fears, and given us a way to share topics we weren't ready to bring up in face to face conversation. But I wasn't thinking this way. Daily survival was the goal. I considered it a win if I got through the day just being able to eat like a "normal" person.

It's been over six years since this experience, and my daughters are still struggling a little bit. Just as I was triggered by my diagnosis, and it brought back a lot of the feelings I had during my mom's cancer diagnosis, my daughters still get triggered as well. If one of their friend's parents is diagnosed with cancer, it brings it all back for them. If I get sick, even just a stomach bug, they remember when I was sick from the chemotherapy and it takes them back to that scary time in their lives. I now understand the power of post-traumatic stress disorder. However, I believe they will each get to a place where they're able to release these negative memories and tap into all the positive lessons we learned as a result of what our family went through when I was diagnosed.

. . . .
WORDS OF WISDOM FROM MOM, 1990

Stress can make anyone crazy. In today's world we
all strive to accomplish and do a great deal. However, we
must make time to relax and unwind. Make time
for yourself. Just find one sport to unwind daily.
It's very important because it helps you to regroup,
to revive yourself and to relax, not to mention
how healthy it is for your body.

It's a gift to learn how to help yourself deal with the challenging situations life can sometimes toss your way. I didn't really have these skills initially. I tried to deal with my anxiety by lying in bed and Googling the stages of breast cancer. I memorized treatment plans, statistics, and life expectancy charts, which didn't help very much. Instead, it made the situation worse. Since then, I've had counseling, read a ton of self-help books, gone to meditation retreats, taken classes, and explored various ways to manage and deal with the uncertainties of life. I learned how to stay grounded by cultivating a daily spiritual practice, and this has changed my life.

The key is to commit to finding what works and feels the best *to you*.

Just as my mom indicated above, exercise is an important way to unwind. When we move our bodies, we release stress and anxiety. I try to do some form of exercise on most days. If you haven't found a form of exercise you enjoy, experiment until something speaks to you. Walking in nature is my favorite form of exercise, and I try to get outside a few times a week. I also enjoy yoga and weight lifting. A plethora of research proves that incorporating an exercise routine into your life has significant benefits both mentally and physically.

I'm so grateful I discovered meditation as a way to manage stress, and I can't say enough about this practice. I'm committed to meditating at least one time a day, and can't imagine not having this incredible tool in my life. This doesn't mean that life doesn't sometimes get in the way, and for whatever reason, I don't make the time to meditate. When that happens, I can really feel the difference, and it reaffirms my strong belief in the power of meditation. I love including meditation in the workshops I teach, and I recently became a meditation practitioner. If you haven't meditated before but are open to it, there are plenty of ways to start. Remember, it's a practice, so be patient as you begin to figure out what works for you and speaks to your heart.

When I first started, I found guided meditations on the free app, Insight Timer. That helped me the most because there was a person leading me through the meditation, which was easier than remembering what to do myself. You can even set the timer on the app for the amount of time you want to meditate, or choose a meditation that lasts your desired amount of time. When you first start out, I recommend one to three minutes. If you start out trying to meditate longer, you're probably going to get frustrated. Over time, you can increase the duration and even stop listening to guided meditations and just put on music. The key is to be open to meditating, show up each day, and stick with it. Just dabbling here and there may help you, but you won't be reaping the full benefit.

How Do You Meditate?

- Find a quiet place where you know you won't be disturbed.
- Decide if you're going to use a guided meditation or music and turn it on or get it ready. Think about this before you start, so you don't spend a lot of time trying to figure out what you're going to do.
- Set the timer so you know when to start and finish. Don't try to be an overachiever, especially at first. This is about feeling good about what you're doing.
- Sit comfortably on your yoga mat, meditation pillow, or blanket. I like to sit cross-legged, and I usually rest my hands on my knees with my palms opened and my thumb and index fingers touching.

Sometimes, I bring my hands up to prayer position at chest level.

- Close your eyes.

- Focus on your breathing and try to turn your brain off. I prefer thinking about the air coming in through my nose and going out through my nose, but you might want to repeat phrases such as "positive energy coming in" when you breathe in, and "negative energy going out" when you exhale. Some people like to repeat a prayer or a mantra or even just say one word. The more you practice and play around with different meditations, the more likely it is that you will find what works for you.

- Breathe in and out through your nose. When you inhale, try to take the breath down to your abdomen, expanding your tummy on the inhale and contracting your stomach and pulling the air up and out through your nose on the exhale. This will take a little practice because it's not the way most of us normally breathe. (You might want to put your hand on your tummy, and practice this technique before starting to meditate.) The goal is to slow your breathing and make the inhales and exhales the same length.

- When your mind starts to wander (it will) and you realize you just had a conversation with yourself about everything you need to do, don't get frustrated. Let the thought pass, visualize it moving on, and go back to focusing on your breathing, your mantra, or the person talking if it's a guided meditation.

- 🌿 Be patient with yourself and congratulate yourself for showing up, staying committed, and doing the work.
- 🌿 Keep it up! Try to commit to your meditation practice each day for three minutes. Over time, you will feel the benefits and probably want more. If you don't, no worries, you tried it, and that's amazing. Commitment and consistency are your best friends when it comes to this practice.

My parents loved going camping. When my brother and I were at summer camp, my mom wrote letters to us about going camping with my dad. They enjoyed hiking and sitting by the fire and just spending time in nature. They found it to be relaxing—this was probably their form of meditation. My parents tried to instill their love for camping in me and my brother, and many times over the years we went camping as a family. Of course, it almost always rained. (There wasn't a weather app back then to notify us when it was going to rain.) Not just a little drizzle, but a huge downpour would often occur in the middle of the night when I would have to go to the bathroom. I can't say camping was my favorite thing. "It's all in your attitude," my mom would tell us when we were drenched, everything in the tent was moist, and my dad kept telling us NOT to touch the sides of the tent or it would sag in. We had a lot of laughs in those tents, a lot of fun family moments, and Jon and I tried to replicate this for our kids. It's funny how as an adult I wanted to give this experience to my kids, even though when I was a child I didn't like camping.

Jon and I took Zoe and Avi on several camping trips with friends. We bought all the necessary gear and spent a lot of time and money getting prepared for these outings. Guess what? It almost always rained. And while we still managed to have fun, I've learned that, though I adore hiking and being in nature, my days of sleeping in a tent are over. My family agrees.

CHAPTER 6

Thank Goodness
I Saved the Letters

I wanted to share the letters with someone who would understand how important they were to me. There was only one person who would: my brother Ari. He is three years younger than I am, we're extremely close, and he knows all my secrets. The older we get, the more important our friendship becomes, and the more we lean on one another. We often reminisce about our mom and grandparents, bringing up funny stories or events from our shared past.

On that cold night in January, buzzing from staying up late and reading the bag of letters, I couldn't wait to tell Ari about it. I called him on his cell phone the next morning as I cleaned up the breakfast dishes. I was alone in my house, doing my morning cleanup routine, and he picked up immediately. We'd never talked about the letters or the ziplock bag before, and I wasn't sure if he even knew I had saved all my letters over the years.

"Hey, what's up?" he said in his southern accent. He has the cutest southern drawl and I love it.

"Can you talk?" I asked him. "You're never going to guess what I did last night."

"Sure," he said. "I'm driving to another hospital. What did you do last night?" He chuckled as he said this, thinking I was going to mention something crazy. He's used to never knowing exactly what I'm going to say. Ari is a doctor in Richmond, Virginia, where we grew up, where my dad and stepmother live, and we often talk during the day when he's driving from one hospital to another or when he's between patients.

"I'm not sure I ever told you this," I said, "but I saved almost every letter I ever got from Mom, Dad, and both sets of our grandparents. Most of the letters are from Mom and Grandma Margaret and Grandma Millie. Last night, I finally decided to read them. There are more than a hundred of them, handwritten." I rattled off all of this in one breath. Maybe, I thought, he had other letters and we could read them together.

Silence.

"Did you hear me?" I asked. I wasn't sure if the phone had cut off or if we had bad reception.

He cleared his throat, just like my dad, and then said in a quiet voice, "What letters? I never got any letters."

This time the line was silent, but I was the one who said nothing. After a moment, I said, "What? Of course you got letters. We were both sent the same number of letters."

"I don't think so," Ari said, sounding strange.

"Yes, you did," I continued. "I know you got letters."

"I really don't remember getting any letters," he said.

"Ari," I said. "You know how they would send us letters when we were at camp and then when we went to college? I saved all the letters."

"No," my brother said, "I don't remember getting any letters. And, if I did, I certainly didn't save them."

"I know they wrote you letters," I said. "Because I've read all of the ones I have, and in many of the letters, they would say they had to go and write you a letter, right then."

"Maybe," he said, "but I don't have any letters."

This was not going the way I expected it to go. Of course, he had received letters. There wasn't any favoritism going on here. The last thing I wanted to do was make my brother feel slighted by our relatives who had passed away. Plus, I knew with *certainty* that he'd received them. After going back and forth for what felt like a long time, we both just laughed. I told him all about my experience reading the letters, what they meant to me, and how I couldn't wait for him to read them.

"That's amazing," he said, after I shared a few of the wise words with him. "I really look forward to sitting down and reading all of them."

That first summer at camp I had been so homesick that I probably didn't want to toss anything sent to me from home into the trashcan. I had celebrated my tenth birthday at camp, and wasn't the most responsible kid. I'm guessing I had a ziplock bag and just stuffed the letters I received that summer into it while packing up my stuff. I probably didn't know what else to do with them. The amazing thing is that I kept the bag. I had started a pattern. Each summer, when I received letters from home, I kept them, and when I returned home from camp, and later when I went to college, when I was unpacking my stuff and settling into my room back at home, I would put any letters I received into the original ziplock bag that I kept at home in my closet.

I was sorry my brother hadn't saved any of the letters he received from our family when he was at camp and college, but this is probably the norm. I don't think many people have a ziplock bag stuffed with letters from their deceased family members.

When I was going back and rereading the letters, I found this treasure written by Grandma Margaret, encouraging me to save the letters. Maybe that's where my nine-year-old self got the idea of saving them. I'm not sure, but I'm so very thankful!

. . . .

LETTER FROM GRANDMA MARGARET, 1982

Dear Dara,

By the time you get this letter more than half of your camp time has gone by. Good Girl! I hope you try to enjoy it. Have you gained weight? Eat a good meal every time. Enclosed are some rubber bands you can hold all of your letters together we send to you. Try to smile and enjoy yourself. It's a lot easier than you think! Love you,

Grandma
. . . .

Weeks went by and Avi had not responded to the new mommy-daughter journal I put on her bed. Not only was there no response, but I could feel her pulling further and further away from me, and it broke my heart. I had talked about this with Jon or close friends, but hadn't been able to make any headway. We had conflict over silly, insignificant things; she wouldn't open up to me, and the more I tried, the quieter she got and the more distant she was. We were stuck, and I didn't know what to do. One day, thinking about my frustration with this situation, it was like a lightbulb went off in my head. After reading the letters and hearing my mom's voice, I knew what was creating distance between Avi and me, and I knew what to do about it.

One Sunday, while we were having dinner, Avi sat in her chair sulking, refusing to eat what I made. She was upset because I wouldn't let her go to dinner with her friends. That's when it all came tumbling out. What seemed like an ordinary night became an opportunity for a huge breakthrough for Avi that brought us back together again.

I was tired of arguing with her over insignificant things. It felt like I was the only one putting any effort into our relationship. That evening, she pushed me too far. Instead of shaking it off or letting it go, from reading the letters I had the words of three strong women in my head, cheering me on and telling me it would all be okay.

"You know what," I said, putting my fork down. "For a long time I've been carrying around a lot of guilt for being diagnosed with cancer and for what you were forced to go through. But I'm done. I release the guilt. It wasn't my fault. I can't change what happened. It is what it is, and it's time for you to stop punishing me for it and keeping me at a distance," I said to Avi. "Don't think I don't see it, and it breaks my heart."

I could tell I hit a nerve because her lip started quivering and tears started coming down her face.

I got up out of my chair and went to her. I put my arms around her and rubbed her back. I felt her warm tears on my face, and her body trembled. I held her tighter, this beautiful daughter of mine, connected to me so deeply that her heart had closed at the thought of losing me. She had been pushing me away because she didn't want to risk the heartbreak of that loss. I understood. How I understood.

"Let it out, Avi," I said. "Just let it all out."

I don't know how many minutes we stayed like that, but it felt like a long time. It felt good. It was not only what she needed, but what I needed also—to hold my daughter close like that.

"I'm so proud of you," I said over and over again as I stroked her back. "You're brave to let it out."

She finally looked up and was ready to talk. "The only person I can count on to be there for me is me. Everyone else might leave me and I can't handle it. I can't go through the pain. Not again. So I try to push everyone away."

There it was.

Jon and I looked at one another and kept on talking and trying to get her to let it all out. This was the weight she had been carrying around for five years, and it was too much for anyone to carry, especially an eleven-year-old girl. This was the pain she had tried to push away, but instead she had pushed me away.

"The reality is," Jon said, "everyone is going to die eventually. It's just part of life."

"I hate it," Avi said, through tears.

"Me too," I said. "But the key is to make the most out of the time you have with the people in your life. Not to waste the time." Such simple words to say, but not simple to live.

"You know what, Avi," Jon said. "I worry about something happening to my parents. This is a normal fear, and when you love people so much, of course you worry about them. Another thing, don't think I wasn't scared when Mom was diagnosed. I thought about having to raise you and Zoe by myself, and I was terrified. It was a really hard time for our family, but we got through it. We're lucky."

"As much as I miss my mom," I said to Avi, "I know we did make the most out of the time we had together. That doesn't mean everything was perfect or we didn't argue, because we did. Don't close your heart because you want to protect it. In the end, you will be cheating yourself out of having the best possible relationships you could have with the people in your life."

"Mom tried to do this, Avi. She's been there," Jon said, and we explained how I tried to push him away when my mom passed away and how I was afraid to feel vulnerable and risk getting hurt again, similar to how Avi had been feeling. We told her how there was a time when I was "off my family," how we understood the pain that can come from losing a loved one and wanting to protect your heart from getting broken.

"It does hurt to love and lose," I said. "You know what else? I see now how stuck in grief I was, and how the death of my mom got in the way of my making the most of my life. I know she wouldn't want this for me. And you know what? I would never want this for you."

Once Avi started opening up to us, we had the conversation we needed to have, though none of us had been ready to have it.

"Can I go talk to my grandparents?" Avi said. "I've been shutting them out also, because I don't want it to hurt so much if something happens to them."

"Yes," we said, and gave her the biggest hug ever. Jon and I turned to each other, incredibly moved by what had just transpired.

I'm happy to say that, since that night, our relationship has been thriving. This doesn't mean it's perfect, but there is no such thing.

I was reminded again of how magical moments can be made in the middle of living "normal" life.

. . . .

WORDS OF WISDOM FROM MOM, 1986

Humans have the capacity to survive and move forward.
We can overcome difficult times.

I used to worry that I wouldn't be able to handle it if something happened to my parents. What I had to learn is that worrying about what might happen doesn't prevent things from happening or keep people safe and protected. For me, worrying was a form of control. Subconsciously, I thought that, if I was worrying about something, I could prevent it from happening. This isn't how life works. Worrying took up a lot of energy I could have spent on creating and evolving. If we want to make the most of our lives, we have to be resilient and push ourselves through the challenges to get to the other side.

Just turn on the news tonight, and look at all the challenges people are forced to endure, in this day, and how they are able to get through it. People are incredibly resilient. You are incredibly resilient. The amazing thing is that we are never alone. People are always there to lean on when life gets overwhelming, but we have to let them in and allow them to help us. Remind yourself of how strong you are when you're faced with a challenging situation. Pay attention to your thoughts, and tell yourself, "I can" get through whatever it is you're dealing with instead of saying, "I can't." Don't be afraid to ask for help when you need it or when you're going through a difficult time. When a situation arises, and you are in the position to help other people, try and make their burden a little lighter.

Our hearts are made for love, for connecting to other people. Open up your heart, let people in, and don't be afraid to face your past, head on, so that you can release whatever is holding you back. You can't enjoy your life to the fullest if you're thinking about what might or might not happen or reviewing your regrets. Have faith in yourself, and trust. This is how we learn and grow. It was in the hardest moments of my life that I grew the most. I just had to get through them and come out the other side to see it.

In the Jewish religion, Friday evening after sundown is the Sabbath. Almost every Friday night, for my entire childhood, we went to Grandma Millie's house in Richmond, Virginia, for Friday night dinner. After Grandfather Kurt passed away, Grandma Margaret moved to Richmond, and she would be at our Friday night dinners as well. Often, other friends would come, and there was always room to squeeze in another person.

It was a fine time for our family to come together. Sometimes, we went to temple for Friday evening services. Other times, we stayed at the house. We almost always had the same dinner: baked chicken, salad, green beans, potato casserole, and challah. For dessert, Grandma Millie always bought a chocolate and vanilla layered cake from Thalhimers Department Store, and we ended the evening snuggled up on the couch watching *Dallas* when it was on. I can't tell you how upset we were when JR was shot. As I grew older, and I wanted to be with my friends on Friday nights, I didn't make it to all the dinners, but Grandma Millie understood. "Come when you can," she would say.

When my kids were growing up, I had good intentions of making Friday night dinner, but it wasn't a priority. I was tired from working all week. Sometimes, we said the blessing over the Shabbat candles or went to temple, but many nights we just went out to dinner with friends and didn't celebrate the Sabbath. This would have been a beautiful ritual from my childhood to continue, but fortunately, both my daughters have a strong sense of family and their faith, which is what these weekly dinners gave me.

What is most important is to figure out how you can connect with your family, establishing ways that work for you and your schedule, and to make these a priority. Our society is incredibly busy and fast paced, and many people feel disconnected and alone. Figure out a way for your friends and family to frequently connect, intentionally. It matters, maybe even more than you realize.

Here are several ways you can connect with your friends and family:

- Have a weekly or monthly potluck lunch or dinner. Make it less about the food and more about a fun night with your favs.
- Take a weekly walk or hike, trying different places. This way you'll get in exercise, spend time in nature, all while making time for the people you care about.
- Schedule a game day or night. Mahjong is my favorite and I play every Tuesday at 12:00 p.m. I look forward to it every week.
- Commit to having a movie night. It's always fun to snuggle up on the couch, make a fun snack, and watch a movie.

- Plan a weekend brunch. I love getting together for brunch because it's easier to prepare the food and you still have the whole day ahead of you.
- Create a supper club or cocktail club with your friends. We've participated in both, and it was a great way to see a lot of people once a month.
- Consider an annual family trip. We go to the beach with my side of the family each year, and have been doing this for around ten years.

CHAPTER 7

You're Going to Summer Camp

T he first time I went to sleepover camp I was nine years old, it was for a month, and I didn't want to go. My parents strongly encouraged me to go, and since it was a Jewish camp, they were sure I would love it. They were wrong.

My parents decided that Camp Blue Star in North Carolina was the best camp for me. It was the same camp my dad and uncle had attended when they were kids, and they wanted me to have the opportunity to be with other Jewish kids from around the country.

Back then, the shortest amount of time a camper could attend Camp Blue Star was a month, and once my parents decided I was going, I was going. There wasn't a "starter session" or a "weekend at camp." A month seemed really long to me, but my parents and grandparents said the time would go by fast and I wouldn't want to leave. The fact that I didn't know any other girls my age who would be there at the same time didn't seem to be an issue for anyone except me.

I spent the night before I left packing, making sure I had everything on the list, and labeling all my belongings. The next morning, my parents, brother, and I piled into our car and headed for

Hendersonville, North Carolina. We drove most of the way and stayed overnight in a hotel close to the camp. We had to be there early the next morning, and my parents were excited. My dad couldn't wait to see "his" camp again, after all of these years, and show it to my mom. But in the hotel room that evening I decided I couldn't go to camp. A month was just too long and I didn't want to go.

"Please don't make me go," I begged my parents.

"You'll love it," they said. "You won't want to come home."

"It's too long," I cried. "I can't do this."

"Yes you can," they said. "They'll take good care of you. It's normal to have butterflies. You're just excited about all the fun you're going to have."

There was no going back. They wouldn't budge and they were sure everything would be fine. I had never been away from them for more than a couple of days and this didn't seem like a great idea. I could hardly sleep. Then I heard the phone ringing and the wakeup call indicating that it was time to get up, get dressed, and head to camp.

There wasn't much to pack, since my trunk and all my belongings were still in the car, including my sleeping bag, poncho, flashlight, and cup. My name was written with a Sharpie in everything I owned. We checked out of our hotel room and headed to breakfast.

"You need to eat a good breakfast," my dad said. "You don't want to get to camp hungry."

There was nothing I wanted to do less than eat, and the smell of all the fried food being served at the restaurant was the last thing I needed. After watching my brother stack up his plate with pancakes, eggs, and potatoes, I ran out of the restaurant because I felt like I was going to vomit. I went to the parking lot and waited by the car, crying and wondering what I could do to get out of going to camp, while my family enjoyed the "all you can eat" buffet.

They weren't happy that I left the restaurant, and discussed this when they got to the car. "Was it necessary to make a scene?" my mom said. "You'll be fine once we drop you off and leave. Within five minutes you will have lots of new friends and love camp." They kept saying this over and over again. They were so sure.

They were wrong. I didn't like Camp Blue Star.

To say I was homesick is an understatement. The first night I was okay, but then it hit me. I was going to have to be at this camp for four weeks. I cried all the time. At first, the other girls in my cabin were very nice to me, gave me hugs and comforted me. But after a while, they stopped. Even the counselors eventually lost their patience with me.

I didn't have the friends my parents promised me I would have. What nine-year-old girl wants to hang around with a crybaby all the time?

Fortunately, there were many activities to do during the day to keep us busy, and most of the other kids were very happy and having fun. There was nature, arts and crafts, swimming in the lake, and hiking. Camp Blue Star was one big party for all the other kids. One activity was play practice, and it was required. Everyone in my unit was going to be in a big play the last week of camp, and we would perform it for the whole camp before we went home. I was in the chorus, and to get ready and make sure we knew the songs, we went to play practice several times each week for the whole four weeks. The play was *Free to Be You and Me*. It sounded like fun, until I went to the first play practice. We were all given sheets with the various songs, which we would continue to fine-tune and practice at most rehearsals throughout the summer. The song I remember best was called, "Parents Are People."

What this meant is that each time I went to play practice, several times a week, I would sing about mommies and daddies. While everyone else loved the music and the song, going to play practice didn't distract me from being homesick. Instead, I would sing and think about how much I missed my family. I literally spent almost every play practice crying. It was horrible. Tears would stream down my face as we sang about mommies and daddies.

I didn't want to stay at camp, and begged my counselors to let me go home. I wrote letters to my parents and grandparents asking them to pick me up. They wouldn't cave. I later learned that my dad was extremely homesick the first summer he attended Camp Blue Star, and instead of forcing him to stick it out, my grandparents drove to Hendersonville and picked him up. My dad had always regretted their decision, even though he went back to Camp Blue Star each summer after that. He felt like they should have taught him that he was strong enough to handle any situation he had to face. What this meant for me was there was no way in hell I was getting picked up that summer. Seems the apple didn't fall far from the tree.

. . . .

LETTER FROM GRANDMA MILLIE, 1982

Dearest Dara,

I received your letter today and Grandpa and Grandma must have read it over five times. We are so happy you are at camp and very proud of you. Dara at camp! My, you are such a big girl. We are all fine. It is very hot here and it is hard to take. I wish I were at camp! Today was my last day of work for three weeks and I feel happy about that. I need a good rest. Keep writing us. I get a thrill when I get a letter from you because you are my favorite girl. Have fun and before you know it we will be hugging you.

Love, Grandma

The crying continued, day after day, play practice after play practice. One afternoon, tired of my crying, my counselors took me to see the director, known as Uncle Herman. I sat in Uncle Herman's office, and he asked me about being homesick. Then, he took out a "magic wand" and waved it over my head. "Abracadabra," he said. "You aren't homesick anymore." Sadly, this brilliant tactic didn't work. It just made me cry more.

Apparently, my parents received a letter from the camp about this little situation. For some reason, my dad saved the letter and I found it when I was writing this book. One night, as I was falling asleep, something told me to get out of bed, go into the kitchen, and look in the bottom drawer of a black cabinet I keep in my kitchen. I couldn't remember the last time I looked for anything there. Inside, I found a folder in my dad's handwriting labeled "Dara." Was it another moment of divine intervention? I don't know, but I loved it.

This treasure was inside the "Dara" folder:

. . . .

LETTER FROM THE CAMP DIRECTOR, 1982

Dear Terri and Harry [my mom and dad],

We welcomed our campers last Monday and have gotten off to a wonderful second session. However, Dara's counselors tell us that Dara is having a little difficulty adjusting to camp life. In case you receive a letter to this effect, please know that we are aware of the situation and we are working very hard to overcome this little adjustment period. As it is still early in the session, by the time you receive this letter, the temporary homesickness could be over.

It is not unusual at all for campers to miss their home and family. In fact, it would be surprising if they don't. However, this is one of the overall goals of all good camps, to help your children to learn how to "be on their own," to make them independent, and to teach them how to overcome some of the little everyday problems that come up in life.

Please be assured that at this state it is not serious and we promise to keep you informed. This is merely to alert you in case you should receive a letter mentioning the homesickness. If you have any questions, do not hesitate to let us hear from you.

Sincerely, Herman

It was a really hard summer, but I got through it, grew up a little bit more, and ended up going back to Camp Blue Star the following year (with friends from home) and then Camp Ramah. I attended summer camp almost every summer, year after year, going for as long as eight weeks at a time. I still cried when it was time to say good-bye to my parents, and never wanted to eat breakfast that morning, but I fell in love with camp and I cherish my memories. I usually cried more when it was time for me to say good-bye to my camp friends, because I knew I would miss them so much. Fun fact: Jon and I discovered that he went to Camp Blue Star also, and he was just as homesick as I was.

When it was time for our daughters to go to camp, many years later, I received the same kind of homesick letters from them. Since technology had advanced, sometimes these letters were sent to me in a fax, and I couldn't help but laugh at being on the receiving end of a homesick letter. Often, I had access to a website where the camp would post daily pictures taken of all the campers. I would pore over these files, looking for a picture of Zoe or Avi, and I felt so happy when I found one. As they got older, they were allowed to have their phones at camp, and we texted each other. Sadly, my daughters don't have a ziplock bag of letters sent to them at camp.

I'm not sure that I would have this bag of letters, containing beautiful words from the people who loved and raised me, if I hadn't gone to Camp Blue Star.

WORDS OF WISDOM FROM
GRANDMA MARGARET, 1982

Make sure you are going to the toilet regularly.
If you have trouble, you have to mention it
to the counselor. It is very important.

I love everything about this quote because I can't tell you how many times my grandmother wrote this to me. She was very concerned with my bowel movements and was always asking me, and each of her five grandchildren, if we were pooping regularly. Grandfather Kurt was a doctor, and she served as his nurse for many years, although she never had any formal medical training. Fortunately, I never had to seek help from a counselor for any toilet issues. Can you imagine a nine-year-old girl going to a counselor and saying, "My elimination doesn't seem to be quite regular. I'm going to need some help with my constipation." Yeah, I don't think so.

WORDS OF WISDOM FROM MOM, 1982

Lice! Don't use anyone's brush or hat.
Even the best camps get it too!

I laughed out loud when I saw this the night I was sitting in my den, reading the letters. I don't remember having lice at camp, being checked for lice, or anyone in my cabin having it. I assume there must have been a letter sent to parents from the camp. Unfortunately, each of my daughters has had her share of lice, and it isn't anything I would wish on my worst enemy. Dealing with lice is exhausting because of all the work it takes to get rid of it. As my mom said, I always told my girls not to share brushes with their friends. Sometimes they listened, sometimes they didn't.

WORDS OF WISDOM
FROM GRANDMA MILLIE, 1982

Enjoy junk food only when you're at camp.

It's not like I didn't grow up on my share of junk food: Little Debbie cakes, sugary cereal, bologna sandwiches, Pringles, and Sara Lee Pound Cake. I laughed when I read this quote. I wouldn't say I was raised on a particularly healthy diet, but back then, we didn't have the information we have now. Camp food wasn't memorable, but I do remember getting ice cream and candy bars from the camp store and having cookies often. At home, frozen fish sticks, green beans out of a can, and mac and cheese were some of my favorites. I'm fairly certain my daughters have never had a fish stick or a lot of the other "wholesome" food I grew up on.

. . . .

WORDS OF WISDOM FROM
GRANDMA MARGARET, 1985

Watch out for your things. It is good to make order
once a day, so you know where everything is.

Grandma Margaret was very organized. Whenever I visited her, her home was always clean and clutter free, and everything had its designated place. There probably weren't any "junk drawers" in her home! When she traveled, she even had a system she used to keep her clothing organized. She would roll her clothes to keep them wrinkle free, and this allowed her to fit many items into a small suitcase. She also used shower caps around her shoes to keep everything clean and neat. She would be impressed to learn that I kept the letters with me through all of my moves, but it's not because I was organized or knew where everything was. She and my grandfather Kurt had the neatest handwriting. They would buy games and art supplies for their five grandchildren, and kept a game closet in their home. My grandfather read the directions for each game, and then, to make it easier for us to follow them, he listed on an index card the steps we would need to take. He taped this version of the directions to each of the games. This way we could play without having to read the long pamphlet that came inside each game.

WORDS OF WISDOM FROM MOM, 1982

Remember to let your positive attitude
be a part of each day. Then, whatever
you're experiencing will work for you.

I've learned how to cultivate a positive attitude through the years, but until I read the letters, I had forgotten how positive my mom was, how she made up her mind to face challenges with an optimistic attitude. I had forgotten her pep talks. Reading each of her letters was like getting one of those pep talks because I could hear her voice in my mind. And I could close my eyes and see her smile. I sure have missed getting those pep talks, but having the letters allows me to hit the bag every time I feel I'm in need of one. I realize I've been giving these same pep talks to my daughters, over the years. Even though my daughters don't realize it, my mom's words travel through me to them, connecting us even more. There's nothing like knowing your mom is proud of you and cheering you on.

I AM MY MOTHER'S DAUGHTER

. . . .
WORDS OF WISDOM
FROM GRANDMA MILLIE, 1988

Camp is not the Hilton Hotel. The purpose is to learn
so that you can be a leader when you come home.

I'm assuming this was written in response to a letter I sent to my grandparents complaining about the accommodations at camp. My camps weren't fancy. It was really all about the friendships we made and the growing we did, even when we didn't realize we were learning and growing.

. . . .
WORDS OF WISDOM
FROM GRANDMA MARGARET, 1982

Do not pack any wet clothing into your suitcase.
Keep them separate; but do not forget
to take them home.

I remember how unhappy my mom was when we left wet towels in our pool bag and forgot about them for days so that everything got moldy. The above message was ingrained in my head, over and over again. I probably should have done a better job making sure my kids understood this when they went to camp. I can't tell you how often a bag of wet, yucky, bad smelling clothes came home from camp because something wet was put into the bag and then sealed up. I love that my grandma was thinking about these kinds of things enough to want to take the time to write to me and tell me what I needed to do. She knew I could use a little refresher.

My grandmothers didn't always get along with one another, and my mom often found herself in the middle of their little squabbles. Millie and Margaret were from two different worlds, one from Berlin, Germany, one from Ellenville, New York. While they were both focused on their families and had a strong faith, Millie was fun loving and full of laughter, and Margaret was formal and serious. My grandfathers, Kurt and Bubs, got along well and had a lot of mutual respect, but after their deaths, Millie and Margaret, both living in Richmond and moving in the same social circles, had frequent spats, usually over nothing important. My mom would often get to hear each side of the story, and this caused her a lot of stress. She strongly disliked having to spend time on the phone with each of them when they were in the middle of an argument, and eventually told them not to contact her when she was at work unless it was an emergency.

As my grandmothers got older and it became harder for them to host big family dinners and holidays, we often gathered at my parents' house for these celebrations. Plus, my parents' house was like Switzerland, and Millie and Margaret tended to behave there. Since they both loved to cook, they always brought homemade food to contribute to the dinner. Most of the time everyone played nicely in the sand box, but there was one evening when they both showed up to my house with their assigned dishes, and the food wasn't the only thing getting heated in the kitchen.

Millie had been assigned to make matzah balls, which she was good at, and Margaret had been assigned to make the chicken soup that the matzah balls would be put into. Both can be a lot of work to make, and my mom thought it would be easier for them to each just make one dish. Instead of sticking to their assignments, they had both gone ahead and made matzah balls and chicken soup. You wouldn't think this was a big deal, but it was because they each wanted everyone at the dinner to have some of *their* soup and *their* matzah balls, and a loud conversation about this was going on in the kitchen. They didn't want their soups co-mingled or the balls mixed together in the same pot. I'm guessing they wanted everyone to be able to tell whose soup and matzah balls were better. They each secretly wanted people to say, "Yours is better than hers."

I was in the kitchen with my mom and grandmothers, keeping my mouth shut and watching this play out. It was like a reality TV show before reality TV was a phenomenon. Finally, my mom said, "I'm not serving everyone different bowls of soup. This is ridiculous." She said, "We aren't doing this." My mom agreed to leave the pots separate on the stove, but when it was time to serve the soup, she gave everyone a little soup and a matzah ball from each pot.

This is just one example of many that I share to remind you that every relationship has challenges. We don't always get along with our family, but we have a choice. We can look for things to get worked up over, or we can accept one another, flaws and all, and make the most of our time together. When disagreements and arguments come up, having the ability to move forward, without holding a grudge or bringing it up again, is important to building your relationships. I know both my grandmothers really cared for one another, but they didn't always bring out the best in each other.

CHAPTER 8

You Can't Hide from Grief

It is not easy to love someone and then lose them, and be forced to live in the world without that person. For me, it's been hard to accept that death is part of life. For years, grief was in my life, my silent companion. It was with me when I opened my eyes in the morning; it went along for the ride as I traveled through my day, and was there at night when I returned home to my family. Here's the sneaky part about grief: you don't always know it's there.

Grief is there when you least expect it. After the tears. After the yelling. After the sadness. After the anger. The loss of my mom, and later the loss of my grandmothers, brought on wave after wave of grief. I've learned you can't run from grief, and a girl can only distract herself for so long. Plus, it takes a lot of energy to try and outrun feelings of grief. Eventually, everyone has to face their losses. After a lot of work, I've learned to live in this world without my mom, my grandmothers, and everyone else I have loved and lost. Not by choice, but by necessity.

I remember a "normal" night, many years ago, when a wave of grief came out of nowhere and hit me harder than I could have imagined. I was cleaning up the kitchen after dinner, when Jon came into the kitchen looking for office supplies.

"Do you have any labels?" he asked.

"I think I have some in here," I said as I opened a "junk drawer," and fished around. I didn't find labels. Instead, I found my mom's leather wallet and daily calendar from 1999, the year she passed away. Don't ask me how it got into my house or into that drawer. All I know is that I was having a normal evening, cleaning my kitchen with plans to make a hot cup of tea and relax in front of the TV, until I wasn't.

"What is this?" I said to Jon. I took a deep breath, walked over to the kitchen island, sat down on a bar stool, and held the leather wallet in my hand.

"What's wrong?" Jon asked. "What happened?"

"It's my mom's," I said. "Her wallet and calendar."

"Are you okay?" he asked.

I have to say, he's incredibly understanding and supportive when I'm hit with a wave of grief. He is blessed to have both of his parents, and even though he hasn't personally experienced this kind of loss, he never tries to tell me my feelings aren't valid. He has learned that the best thing he can do for me is give me a hug, hold my hand, and listen as I release any sadness that wants to come out. His calm manner has been a gift to me over the years.

I opened up the wallet and saw three small square pictures, stuffed in the back. There was a picture of my dad, one of my brother, and one of me. Seeing this brought tears to my eyes. She loved us so much that she carried our pictures around in her wallet. I continued looking through the wallet, where I found her license, a few old credit cards, and her 1999 calendar. I opened up the calendar and flipped through the pages, starting at the beginning of 1999. Each day was full. There were meetings and appointments, presentations she gave, and classes she taught. She had lunch with friends, yoga classes, and dinner plans. Since I lived out of town, in North Carolina, each weekend Jon and I were scheduled to visit was marked in big letters: "Dara and Jon visit." It was obvious she looked forward to seeing us.

I thought, *This calendar belonged to a person living a big life. A happy life. A meaningful life.*

I continued flipping through the months, until I got to THE appointment. The one where everything changed. The one where she went in for a checkup, which led to more appointments and eventually the final heartbreaking diagnosis: stage four reoccurring melanoma. It was so strange to see it all in black and white, how it played out in time, because I knew the ending. I continued flipping through the calendar. After the date of THE appointment, there were only blank pages, except for doctor's appointments. And then the writing stopped. I guess my dad started keeping track of her medical schedule.

My heart sank. The tears streamed down my face. I hadn't been blindsided by grief in a long time. I didn't want it now. Not tonight. I was just looking for labels.

Grief doesn't care. When a song or a comment or an object triggers it, I've learned to let myself feel whatever emotions come up, not judge myself for being upset or for crying, and give myself permission to feel the pain. While time has helped, grief still comes up every now and then, and I imagine it always will. In some ways, I don't want it to ever stop. I don't want the distance between when I last saw my mom and the present moment to become so great that I don't remember the details or my feelings start to fade.

Since my mom was young when she passed away, it felt like we had been cheated. I would see friends with their mothers, especially when they had a new baby and their moms would go and stay at their home to help. I didn't have patience for my friends who would complain about their mothers. "She's so annoying," a friend would say about her mom. "She comes to my house and bosses me around like a child," or, "My mother doesn't understand what it's like to work and have kids. She's always telling me what I should do instead of accepting me for who I am and the choices I've made." Each time, I wanted to turn to my friend and shout, "Are you kidding? Do you know how lucky you are to have your mom?" I couldn't do this, of course, because they wouldn't have understood. Plus, I wanted them to feel comfortable opening up and being honest around me. What made it hard was about me, not them.

My brother's wedding was another special occasion that she was cheated out of attending. We didn't talk about it, because it was so near the surface that the tears would have started falling, and wouldn't have stopped. I like to think the unexpected rainbow that appeared right before the ceremony was her way of letting us know she was there. When my kids had their Bat Mitzvahs, my mom wasn't there to celebrate with us. But it wasn't just the big moments; it was the normal day to day living she really missed out on.

My dad waited a year after my mom passed away before he started dating other women. He felt this was a respectable amount of time. My brother and I appreciated this. When the year was up, we knew that friends were introducing him to single Jewish women. I remember the day my dad called to tell me he was getting married to my now-stepmother, Lois. I knew he had a "woman friend," but I had no idea they were as serious as they were. We were out of town with friends when he called my cell phone.

"Lois and I are engaged," he said.

"What?" I said, and then recovered quickly. "Congratulations." I remember talking for a few minutes and then congratulating Lois, whom I had met just a few times. When we got off the phone, I spent the rest of the afternoon crying and feeling sad. I was stunned. It's not that I didn't like Lois—I didn't really even know her. It didn't matter who it was. I didn't want a stepmother because I didn't want my mom to not be alive. It was hard to watch my dad going through the wedding festivities and building a new life with someone other than my mom.

When my mom was in the hospital and things weren't going the way we had planned, she turned to me and said, "Be nice to your father's wife. Don't cause any trouble." It was just the two of us in the room, and my dad was on the way to the hospital with relatives who came to visit my mom. Now I know that they wanted to say "good-bye" to my mom, but we didn't talk about this. Instead, we pretended they wanted to have a friendly visit with her. We were enjoying our vacation in denial. We had taken my mom to the hospital because we thought she was dehydrated again and wanted her to get fluids.

"What are you talking about?" I asked my mom after she mentioned my dad having a new wife. It was the only time she hinted about her possible death. She said this immediately after a doctor had come into the room to say that he couldn't operate on the brain tumor that was on her cerebellum. This news had been hard to hear and to process, especially without my dad and brother there. Obviously, a lot more than dehydration was going on.

"I'm so sorry, Terri," the doctor said. "There's nothing we can do. I can go in and relieve some of the pressure, to extend your life so you will see your grandchild. You have a pregnant daughter, don't you?"

"That's me," I said. I was sitting there, barely understanding what he had just said, and he couldn't see the basketball in my tummy. I hadn't gained a lot of weight. Watching someone you love spiral downward can kill an appetite.

"When are you due?" the doctor asked me.

"In about six weeks," I said.

"Six weeks," he said, and I could tell he was calculating something. "That should be okay."

I didn't know what to do or how to handle the situation, so I just said, "Let's wait for Dad to get here; he'll know what to do. Just eat your lunch. That brownie looks really good."

"I feel like I want to cry and be a little sad," my mom said. "Your father deserves to be happy and I want him to start a new life."

It's hard for me to write this.

How I wish I had handled this situation better. If I could go back, I would have held her hand, told her how much I loved her, said something meaningful, and even allowed myself to open up and talk about how terrified I was to be losing her. But I wasn't ready to admit that she was going to die and there wasn't anything we could do to prevent it. Saying, "Eat your brownie" was the best I could do.

I've played this situation in my head over and over again for years, each time feeling worse and worse about what I *didn't* say and what I *should* have said. However, I learned that reliving the past and playing it over and over again in my mind doesn't help. The best way to handle regret about the past is to give ourselves a dose of grace and forgiveness. "Let it go," I imagine my mom saying to me. "It doesn't matter." One conversation doesn't define a relationship.

I often didn't feel comfortable being alone with my mom towards the end of her life. I was afraid something would happen and I wouldn't know what to do. Maybe I was trying to shield myself from having serious conversations that I wasn't ready to have. But I have tried to honor the words she said to me that day, regarding my dad. I've tried to behave and not cause any unnecessary drama with my stepmother. It has not always been easy. Lois and I are very close, and she is a blessing to our family, but I still wish my mom were alive.

"I wish we could have met Grandma Terri," my daughter Avi said one day out of the blue, completely innocently, as little kids often do. We were in Richmond, visiting my dad and Lois, and in the kitchen making breakfast. "But then we wouldn't have Lois, and I love Lois."

I understand Avi. It's complicated for all of us.

I have to give my dad a lot of credit here, because he has led by example. Since marrying Lois, he has included my Grandma Millie and my mom's family in every holiday celebration and family get-together. To her credit, Lois welcomed them into her home. In return, Grandma Millie and Lois developed a beautiful friendship; Lois even took her to appointments at times, and helped her with her finances. Everyone was willing to open their hearts and let one another in. It's a reminder that love doesn't have boundaries.

What I've learned from personal experience and from talking with so many people is that you can't run from grief. You can try to distract yourself and pretend it isn't there, keep yourself busy and try not to think about it, but this will only delay the inevitable. It also doesn't matter how old you are when you lose someone you love. Whether you're a twenty-something daughter trying to move forward after the loss of your mom or a seventy-something widow trying to figure out how to live in the world without your partner, losing someone you love hurts. It takes time to learn how to deal with the pain and move forward. It takes a willingness to allow yourself to feel pain, let it move through you, and then commit to moving forward, remembering that it's okay to be happy again.

I try to channel my fear of death into loving better, by showing the people I care about how much they mean to me. I realize that I can try to protect my heart by holding back my love, just as Avi did, or I can decide to enjoy each and every day with the people I'm blessed to have. Living fully and loving deeply is the secret. It's been a journey for me to learn this, but I'm very grateful that I have.

. . . .

WORDS OF WISDOM FROM MOM, 1993
(MY COLLEGE YEARS)

I hope you appreciate how fortunate you are.

Gratitude. There's nothing that has helped me more in finding peace. Living with gratitude means counting your blessings. It means focusing on what you have, or had, not what you don't like or have lost. I didn't always understand what it meant to live a life of gratitude, until I was trying to help myself deal with cancer.

When I started to take time each day to acknowledge the good in my life, even in the midst of a crisis, it made a big difference.

I wish I had always lived my life with gratitude. It would have helped me find peace sooner after my mom passed away. Instead of being laser focused on what I had lost, I could have thought about how lucky I was to have had my mom as long as I had her. Find your blessings, count them, and hold onto them with both hands.

Research indicates that people who take the time to count their blessings, each day, are happier and more joyful than people who don't. Starting a daily gratitude practice is easy; it just takes commitment and consistency. If you don't have a daily gratitude practice, I encourage you to consider starting one.

How to Incorporate a Daily Gratitude Practice into Your Life

When you're just starting out, it's easiest to have a gratitude journal. Get a notebook and designate it solely for this purpose. Each day, commit to writing down three things in your life you are grateful for. How easy is that? It's super simple, but it helps you shift your mindset from counting your problems to counting your blessings. Decide if you want to do this in the morning, evening, or both, and do it. Eventually, you will probably find yourself traveling through your day thinking about everything you're grateful for, and it's a beautiful way to live. I tend to do this before I even get out of bed in the morning, and then again before I go to sleep. I like thinking about what I'm grateful for before I start my day, and then at the end of the day.

. . . .

WORDS OF WISDOM FROM MOM, 1992

Love life, enjoy life and make each day
so special that you see the beauty.

It all comes down to letting yourself enjoy life, whatever your circumstances, and deciding to make the most of each day. There is so much beauty in this world, but it's easy to forget to open your eyes and see it. Believe me, I've wasted many sacred moments fretting about whatever wasn't working in my life. But as my mom said, "Love life," the actual gift of being alive. She cherished life with all her heart. She would take a sip of orange juice, enjoy and savor the taste, and smile and say, "I love being alive." I know she learned this from her dad, my grandfather Bubs, and she always said that he did this when he drank his morning orange juice. Let yourself feel the joy of being alive, and recognize that your time on earth is limited.

. . . .

WORDS OF WISDOM FROM
GRANDMA MARGARET, 1985

Be rather selective with whom you become really
close with. It is good to be friendly with everybody,
but you know what I mean, darling.

You are who you surround yourself with. If you spend a lot of time with positive people, you're more likely to have a positive mindset. If you spend time with negative people, their negatively will probably rub off on you. Pay attention to who you spend your time with, and don't be afraid to make changes if you feel it is necessary.

When my kids were younger, I always told them to make sure they chose their friends wisely. I knew how important their friends were and what a big impact their friends would have on them. If they hung around with kids who made good choices, I recognized my kids would be more likely to make good choices. Grandma Margaret was right. It doesn't cost anything to be nice and kind to other people and friendly to everyone you come into contact with. However, that doesn't mean you have to let everyone into your inner circle. Make sure you spend time with people who love and care about you, unconditionally, and who make you feel good about yourself. If there are people in your life who make you feel badly, judge you, or put you down, consider spending less time around them. I've learned that not everyone is meant to travel through my life with me. I gave myself permission to release relationships that weren't helping me be the best version of myself, or with people I didn't feel I was in alignment with. While it can sometimes be hard to do this, remember that when you let go of toxic friendships, you're opening up space to bring new friendships into your life. How beautiful!

As close as I was to my mom, there was one topic we never discussed: sex. When I was in middle school, I remember my parents setting up the Monopoly game, a game I loved, and inviting me to play with them. Only, instead of playing Monopoly, we very uncomfortably discussed the birds and the bees, in under fifteen minutes, and that was that. It was painful for all of us.

When I was in college, I decided I needed to go on birth control pills. Of course, my sorority sisters were more than happy to bring me up to speed on this topic, and I was instructed to visit the health center, meet with a doctor, and be given a prescription for birth control pills. The monthly expense for these pills was four dollars, which would be billed to my dad. "Dara," my dad said one day when we were talking on the phone, "what is this reoccurring expense we keep getting each month?" I paused for just a moment and then was hit with brilliance. "It's allergy medicine," I said. "My allergies are really bad here, and I keep having issues." That made perfectly good sense, and he was satisfied. Plus, why would his sweet daughter lie to him? The week before my wedding, I was running around with my mom and we were in the car at a stop light. Out of the blue, she said, "Have you given any thought to birth control?" I laughed and said, "Remember that monthly four-dollar charge? Instead of allergy medicine it was actually for birth control pills. I've been having sex with Jon for years." She laughed and that was that. No need to discuss sex.

Jon and I tried to talk to Zoe and Avi about sex, starting when they were young, so that we could discuss this topic openly and honestly as they got older. I didn't want a replay on the Monopoly game. But when the girls were really little, we had a situation. I had gone to a meeting one evening and left Jon in charge. I wasn't prepared for what I walked in on a couple of hours later.

"I'm home," I said, walking into the sunroom where everyone was hanging out watching something on the computer.

"What are you watching?" I asked.

That's when I saw it.

"What is this?" I asked, confused as Zoe and Avi stared at the computer screen while jumping around.

"The girls asked how babies are made while you were gone," Jon said. "So I pulled up a video about fertilization." On the screen, I saw little sperms in the process of trying to penetrate an egg.

"Are you kidding? I was only gone for a couple of hours. Look how young they are. They don't need this now!" I said as I shut the computer screen.

It was obvious they weren't really interested in the boring science lesson going on in front of them.

"God brought you both to us, and we are so thankful," I said, and hugged them both, rolling my eyes at Jon. They were happy with this, and we moved on with the night.

CHAPTER 9

You Need a Nice Jewish Boy

There was one conversation we had throughout my childhood, teen years, and into my college years. It was about who I would and would not marry. It was expected that I would marry an NJB, a Nice Jewish Boy, and the thought of me falling in love with a non-Jewish boy wasn't something my parents or grandparents took lightly. "What if I marry someone who isn't Jewish?" I remember asking one night at the dinner table. I was around twelve and we were having a family dinner with Grandma Millie and Grandpa Bubs at their house, and as usual, the Friday evening conversation was lively and colorful.

"God forbid," Grandma Millie said. "I would plotz." My grandmother was from New York, spoke fluent Yiddish, a kind of Jewish slang, and sometimes tossed these slang words into her daily conversations. I had learned a lot of Yiddish words over the years, but only remembered the colorful ones. When I was little she taught me several cuss words and I felt really special.

"It's just as easy to fall in love with a Jewish boy as it is a non-Jewish boy," my mom said. "Try not to put yourself in a situation where you develop feelings for someone who isn't Jewish."

I remember my parents looking at one another and nodding their heads. I imagine they were thinking, "We handled that well. Crisis averted."

"Marriage is hard enough," my parents told me over the years. "Marrying someone who is Jewish will make it easier. You will have that common bond, you will have grown up the same and have similar values, and you won't have to argue about a Christmas tree."

. . . .
LETTER FROM MOM, 1991

Dearest Dara,

Your life is filled with excitement, fun, and love. We are very proud of you. These are important years and we believe that you are blossoming. It seems that you worry about the future with Jon. Don't. Life has a way of working out. No one can predict what will be. Your dad and I like Jon a great deal. We think he is a fine person, as are his parents. But, you have to decide if he is the right one that you want to live your life with each day. Only you can make that decision, not us. No one is pushing you. So relax, enjoy and allow it to unfold. Stay well, eat enough and have fun!

Love, Mom
. . . .

Since I went to a school that had mostly non-Jewish kids, whenever I went out on a date the question was always, "Is he Jewish?"

not, "Is he nice?" or, "Does he treat you with kindness?" While I know they cared about these things, his religion often seemed like their sole interest. If he wasn't Jewish, God forbid, my parents would shake their heads and look at one another with concern. But if he was Jewish, they would smile and nod their heads approvingly. In these instances, my parents usually knew *something* about his family, who his grandparents or parents were, and what they did. "I'm in high school," I would say. "It's not like I'm going to marry the guy. We're just going to the movies." I couldn't understand why they cared so much, especially since I was so young. "You never know what could happen," they said over and over again. "Don't put yourself in a situation you don't want to be in. There are many nice people in this world, and you don't want to fall in love with someone who isn't Jewish."

Fortunately, I was very active in a Jewish youth group, and this pleased my parents and grandparents. As long as I was with my Jewish friends, it didn't matter what we did, where we went, or how late we stayed out. I was with Jewish kids, and how much trouble could we really get into? I wasn't the only one who was forced to have these conversations. My brother had them with my parents as well, and we would often look at each other and shake our heads as if to say, "What's wrong with these people?" It was our version of *My Big Fat Greek Wedding*.

Now that I'm on the parent side, with two daughters, I find myself asking the same question. "Is he Jewish?" I have asked my kids this many times, even when they were in middle school and started liking a boy. My daughters know Jon and I hope they will marry someone who is Jewish, but we will love and accept whoever they fall in love with. Their happiness is truly what matters most to us.

The world has changed a lot since Grandma Millie and Grandma Margaret were growing up, and since my mom was alive. I have many friends who intermarried and have succesful relationships. Marriage is all about compromising and finding what works in your relationship, and this is something everyone has to figure out for themselves. I would never judge anyone's choice. It's about finding the right person to love and cherish; it's about mutual respect and compromise. Marriage isn't easy for anyone—even for people who have the same religion.

Recently, when Zoe was home from college and talking to me about who she's been hanging out with, I noticed that I didn't even have to ask, "Is he Jewish?" She just filled in this information as she talked to me about her friends. *Wow*, I thought. *We really did a number on her*.

"I'd actually love to have a Christmas tree," Avi said to us one night when Jon and I were talking with her about dating. She was trying to push our buttons. "Maybe I'll marry someone who isn't Jewish just so that I can have a beautiful tree to decorate." When she said this, she looked at us with a smirk, and we tried very hard not to react. "I like the white lights the best," Avi said. Truth be told, we just want our daughters to be happy.

Just because I married a Jewish man doesn't mean we have always agreed on everything having to do with our religion. I was raised in a conservative temple, and Jon was raised in a reform temple. A conservative temple tends to be more strict about following traditions. This difference could sometimes cause a little tension, particularly when it came to attending services at Temple Beth-El in Richmond, Virginia, where my family belongs. There the services were a lot longer than Jon was used to. This was especially true on Yom Kippur, the most sacred holiday in the Jewish religion, where the services often go all day until sunset. Many people fast all day.

"I just can't sit still," Jon would say to me. "I don't want to stay there all day." We often left after the morning service to go home for a couple of hours, and then came back in the late afternoon. I would feel conflicted because I knew that Jon didn't want to sit in temple for so many hours, yet my dad often stayed the whole day.

One Yom Kippur, we were at Temple Beth-El with my dad and Lois, and Zoe and Avi were in the kids' service. Jon got up to leave. "I'm going to stretch my legs," he said. "I just need a break." I shrugged when he said this, and expected him to be gone for a short time. Maybe, I thought, he's checking on the girls, going to the bathroom, or is just going to walk around for a short time. After about an hour, my dad leaned over to me and said, "He probably went to get something to eat." I shrugged and shook my head. Soon after, I looked up, and in walked Jon, with a huge smile on his face. "Oh my God," I remember saying out loud. "Are you kidding?" Jon had taken a walk around the temple neighborhood, wandered over to a fun street with lots of shops and businesses, and ended up getting his hair cut. It was obvious to *everyone*. I was frustrated with him, and knew my dad would be upset. I felt caught in the middle. "Really," I said to him later, "Did you think we wouldn't notice?" He shrugged. "I just can't sit still all day, and I needed a haircut. I wasn't trying to be disrespectful; I just wanted a haircut and happened to find a place to go."

Over the years, little issues have come up regarding how we were going to practice our religion, and we've been able to find solutions and compromises. We just laugh about the haircut story now, after so many years, and have found a good solution. My dad and Lois usually visit us on Yom Kippur. This way, we can all be together, go to our temple, and the service isn't so long. I never expected to have these issues when I married my NJB. I thought we would see everything the same way when it came to our religion and raising Zoe and Avi in a Jewish household. Marriage is challenging, for everyone, even when two people share the same religion.

WORDS OF WISDOM FROM MOM, 1993

We love Jon and his family and you're so lucky
to have met a nice Jewish boy with a wonderful family.
You will have a beautiful life.

This was sent to me before Jon and I got engaged, in a letter written to me when I was in college. I knew how much my parents adored Jon and his family, and this was important to me. Jon fit in well with my family, and our families also got along very well, which made spending time together fun.

I sat there and cried, wearing my beautiful white wedding dress, in the Bride's Room of Temple Beth-El. I had spent many hours playing in this room as a child, pretending to be a bride on my wedding day. It's a little room off of the bathroom at the temple, and is where a bride gets dressed before she walks down the aisle. Many times when I was younger, I would sneak out of services, say I had to go to the bathroom, and find my way into this room, pretending it was my wedding day and I was getting dressed. I would imagine walking down the aisle, greeting my husband who was waiting for me at the end of the aisle, and pretend to kiss him.

Now, it was here.

I had my hair and makeup done, my dress was beautiful, and it was my turn to be the bride in the Bride's Room. But I was feeling emotional and nervous. At age twenty-two, the thought of walking down the aisle in front of so many people terrified me. Plus, for a moment, "forever" seemed like a really long time. I wasn't alone, though. I was surrounded by my best friends, my mom, Grandma Millie and Grandma Margaret, and my soon-to-be mother-in-law, Suzy. They were all taking turns holding my hands, giving me hugs, telling me they loved me.

"Why are you crying?" they all asked me.

"I don't know," I said, through tears laced with laughter. "I guess I'm scared."

"Dara," my mom said, trying to help me, "you're going to mess up your makeup and we won't have time to fix it."

This was a good point; I didn't want to mess up my makeup. But the tears kept tricking down my face. As much as I wanted them to stop, I couldn't.

My grandmothers said, "You love Jon, don't you?"

"Yes," I replied. "Of course."

"And he loves you, right?" They nodded their heads and looked at each other.

"Yes," I replied again, smiling.

"Then dry up those tears and wipe your face," my mom said. "There's really nothing else that matters."

I took a drink of wine and settled in. I breathed a sigh of relief. I was ready to climb the steps of the temple, to the sanctuary, and be escorted down the aisle by my dad, who was waiting for me outside the Brides Room. I was ready to marry Jon. I felt the love of my mom, Grandma Millie, Grandma Margaret, and Suzy, and they were right. It really was just that simple. It's easy to complicate things, but in the end, love really is all that matters.

It's nice when you like and get along well with the family of the person you marry. That saying "You don't just marry the person, you marry the family" is so true. This doesn't mean we haven't had challenges or disagreements or times when Jon and I would argue because of an issue with our extended families. It helped that Jon and I were both raised with a strong sense of family. We both are committed to spending time with our parents, siblings, and extended family, and try to make this a priority. It can be challenging to have to split our time between our families, one in Richmond and the other in North Carolina, especially when it comes to holidays. We've tried to be as fair as possible, alternating between locations and families, trying to keep everyone happy while being true to our own family unit. When we're spending a holiday in North Carolina, I feel my heart tug a little, knowing my Richmond family is all together and feeling left out of that family gathering. I want to be there. I want to be here. I can only be in one place. I've gotten really good at saying, "It is what it is." We're thankful we have two loving families who want to be with us and know it's a good "problem" to have.

If I'm feeling pushback when navigating interactions with extended family members, I remember that the most important thing is for me and my spouse to be on the same page. If we're both feeling the tension, it is important to work it out together, instead of leaning into our respective families, which isn't going to strengthen our marriage. I don't want to divide and conquer; I want to unite and solve. Marriage takes commitment, patience, mutual respect, an open heart, and then more patience.

. . . .
LETTER FROM MOM, 1994

Dearest Dara,

We miss sharing our holiday with you but are glad you had a good one. We are happy and content that you are happy. You will be home for a visit soon! We can hear that you have a full schedule and are busy. Stay well, be happy, and remember how much we love you.

Love, Mom
. . . .

CHAPTER 10

Living with Loss

I
t's hard to lose a loved one. I wish I had some magic words that could take your pain away when someone you love passes away. I've struggled with this pain since the death of my mom, and again with the losses of each of my grandmothers. I've learned that time does help ease the pain, that you can find peace living in a world without your loved one, and that it's okay to move forward and be happy again. If there's anything these strong women taught me in the time we were blessed to have together, it was to cherish each day of my life, to recognize how beautiful the world is, and to not waste the blessings I've been given.

I also know that it is much easier to say these words than to live them.

The first holiday I faced without my mom, Thanksgiving, was incredibly sad. My first Thanksgiving without my mom was also my first Thanksgiving *as* a mom. This strange twist of fate had me bewildered. I was both devastated at my loss and elated at my gain.

Celebrating a holiday for the first time without a loved one is very hard. I remember so vividly how hard that first holiday was, and all the first holidays that came after it: Hanukkah and the Christmas season, and then New Year's Eve.

Then came Rosh Hashanah and Yom Kippur, and with these holidays came Yizkor, a memorial service to remember loved ones who have passed away. I had seen my parents and grandparents sit in this service, remembering their loved ones. But I wasn't ready to do this. Not yet. I celebrated that first Yom Kippur in Richmond with my dad and brother, and it was hard to read the prayers and think about my mom while trying to hold back the tears. It felt like everyone was looking at me, and I didn't want people to see me cry. I felt like I "should" be strong and I didn't want people to see me hurting. Of course, this was all in my head. No one was looking at me and I didn't have to be strong. Finally, I let my tears fall. It was too hard to hold them back and my heart was hurting so much. I didn't care if mascara ran all over my face. I missed my mom. I was now a child attending the Yizkor service for my parent. There's nothing that could have prepared me for hearing my loved one's name called out at temple. *This wasn't supposed to happen,* I thought. *Not to my family.*

Eventually, my family had to begin new traditions and learn to make new memories, without my mom. Trying to figure out how to do this, and hold on to the past at the same time, wasn't easy. Everyone kept telling me, "Once you get past the first year, it will get better." It did get better—many holiday seasons later.

The first anniversary of my mom's death, November fourteenth, was incredibly painful. I didn't know what to do or where to be. Somehow, I ended up in a swimming pool, exercising my way through the pain. I'd always been a swimmer and the feel of the water around my body, giving me a hug, was both comforting and familiar. I looked at my waterproof watch, and swam harder. As the minutes ticked by on the clock, I slammed my arms down into the water harder and harder, tears mixing into the chlorinated water. No one around me knew what I was feeling. To them, I was just a twenty-something adult getting in my daily laps. I got out of the water that evening, took my goggles off, and saw that my eyes were red from crying. I didn't care. I had survived the approximate time, 5:00 p.m., three hundred and sixty-five days after my mom's passing. It was a huge relief.

When I look back on the years since my mom's death, I recognize that I was "stuck" in my grief for a long time. My sadness became all-consuming and got in the way of my enjoyment of the present moment. I allowed grief to take a seat at the head of my table, where it stayed for way too long. I didn't see it then, of course, because I was so stuck in my sadness. You would have thought I'd learn from my mom's death to make the most out of each day.

However, I missed this lesson. This is hard to admit, but it's the honest truth. Instead of seizing each day and living life to the fullest, I wallowed in self-pity. Only after my own experience with breast cancer did I wake up and see how precious life is, and how my mom and grandparents would never have wanted me to let their deaths get in the way of my life. This is such an important lesson, *for all of us.*

When you lose someone you love, intentionally allow yourself time to feel the pain and sadness, but do everything you can to push yourself back into the land of the living. Not only do you deserve this, but your loved one would want you to do this. As the years passed, I tried hard to find ways to bring my mom into my life. And, later, my grandmothers. They are still with me, their presence pulling at my heartstrings, but now in a good way. My dad always says, "Don't be sad it's over; be happy it happened." He typically says this when we've had a visit with each other and I'm sad it's time to say good-bye. These are wise words that I try to remember when I find myself missing my mom. *Don't be sad she isn't here, Dara,* I whisper to myself, *Count your blessings that you had her for as long as you had her.*

. . . .
WORDS OF WISDOM FROM MOM, 1982

It is important to stand on your own two feet.
I promise, Dara, that each time you do something
on your own it will get easier. *Slowly* learn
to do things for yourself.

I had to learn how to deal with my grief by myself. It wasn't something anyone could do for me. Though I read books, went to counselors and groups, and talked with other people who had lost a loved one, I didn't find a formula that I could follow. I wanted someone to tell me exactly what to do to help myself, but everyone is different, every relationship is different, and everyone deals with grief in different ways. There isn't a one-size-fits-all when it comes to mending a broken heart.

While asking for help and talking with others made the journey easier, I had to go through it and do the work myself. And processing grief is work; that's why it's often called "grief work." It's about intentionally thinking about things that might be hard and painful, allowing yourself to feel the pain and sorrow, and then giving yourself permission to release these feelings and find your peace. Moving through it is a process. One day at a time, one step at a time. There were moments when I thought this process was too hard and painful. But just as my mom said, I learned to stand on my own two feet. I learned how to live in the world without her. I learned how to take care of myself and nurture my heart. You can too. It is important to know you can make it through whatever life tosses your way, no matter how hard or challenging your situation is. Remember, it does get easier, over time, and it is empowering to recognize you are strong and can stand on your own two feet.

Each time we do something out of our comfort zone, we develop more confidence and realize we can handle whatever it is that comes our way. This is necessary if we want to live life to the fullest. Plus, most of the time there are exciting new experiences to be had. The world can be your playground, if you let it. It's fun to challenge ourselves and give ourselves permission to try new things. And there is so much beauty and wonder to experience in this life. Remember to go slow, be patient with yourself, and enjoy the journey of self-discovery.

It was the anniversary of my mom's death, and this meant her name would be called out at temple that week. Each year, on the anniversary of a loved one's death, the rabbi reads the person's name and we recite a prayer, the Mourner's Kaddish, a prayer to honor and remember people who have passed away. I received a letter in the mail, informing me of the Friday evening date when my mom's name would be read. What a beautiful way to honor the people you have loved and lost.

"I'm going to temple Friday evening," I said to Jon and Avi. It's the anniversary of my mom's death and I want to say Kaddish. I'd really like it if you would come."

Jon was going to be out of town until late Friday evening, and Avi usually has plans with her friends, but of course, without missing a beat, they committed to coming. Friday afternoon, Avi texted me and told me that several of her close friends wanted to come to temple also, to see what it was all about. She had told them why we especially wanted to go that week. "Is this okay?" she asked.

"Of course," I responded. "How nice."

That evening, we all went out to dinner and then to temple. Towards the end of the service, the rabbi started to talk about people who have come into our lives but are no longer with us. I knew what was coming. It was the twenty-year anniversary of my mom's death, but I never got used to hearing her name called out. The rabbi started reading names, and then said my mom's, "Terri Schuman Hirsch," and I felt myself take a deep breath. Avi took my hand, and we stood up together, along with Jon, who had driven straight to temple from out of town to honor my mom. As we recited the prayer along with the congregation, I turned my head and looked at Avi. She had tears streaming down her face. I let go of her hand and pulled her toward me, hugging her closely as we finished saying the Kaddish together. She felt my sadness and loss.

She also feels connected to my mom. I really couldn't ask for anything more. Any sadness I might have felt was immediately turned to gratitude. I am grateful that she cares. I am grateful she wanted to be there with me. I am grateful to have her. As we sat down together, I thought about how truly blessed I was to have had my mom, and now my two daughters. I was reminded of how connected we all are, in life and death. Instead of sadness, it was love I felt.

Since my children never got to know my mom, I've struggled with how to bring her into their lives. I wanted them to somehow get to know about Grandma Terri. When they were younger, I put a picture of her in each of their rooms, but I wanted them to know more than what she looked like. Though I shared stories and talked about her often, I realized they weren't forming the connection I desired. I remember growing up, hearing about family members who had passed away before I was born, and I never had a true connection to them. I didn't know them or their personalities. To me, they were just old relatives who had passed away. I didn't want this to be the case with my children. I wanted them to really understand who my mom was.

This was before I discovered the letters. Instead of telling my kids about my mom, and trying to explain her personality to them, my kids can read one of the letters she wrote, and get a glimpse of the person she was. Seeing her handwriting and holding a piece of paper she once held in her hands makes the connection stronger. While we have several videos of her at various special occasions, and my kids have watched these, we don't take the time to watch them very often.

Before we discovered the letters, we came up with a tradition that helped us bring my mom into my daughter's lives.

My mom always enjoyed eating ice cream sundaes. She loved nothing more than enjoying a vanilla hot fudge sundae, with as much hot fudge as possible. This was something I knew I could work with. What child doesn't enjoy going out for ice cream or making hot fudge sundaes?

When the kids were really young, we started marking my mom's birthday and the anniversary of her death with ice cream sundaes. Sometimes, I would go all out, buying fun toppings and different kinds of ice cream. Other times, if we were especially busy, we would go to a drive-thru and buy ice cream sundaes on the way home from whatever activity we were engaged in. It didn't matter. They would never get to know her, but I could tell them funny stories or share with them little memories while we enjoyed eating ice cream sundaes. Doing something fun was a way for me to bring my kids and my mom together.

As my kids have gotten older, I see how this tradition has impacted them and how positive it has been for all of us. What I've learned is that it doesn't matter how we do it. The important thing is that we take the time to remember my mom and bring her into our lives. One year, I mentioned this tradition to a close friend, and she surprised me with a set of four ice cream cups and an ice cream scoop. This was an incredible gift, and I will always remember her kindness and generosity.

I know my mom would love everything about this tradition, and this makes me super happy. Keep your loved ones close by finding your ice cream sundaes. Here are other ways you can bring your loved one into your life:

Do Something They Loved

Was there something your loved one especially enjoyed doing? It doesn't matter what it was; try to come up with something he or she adored and go and do it yourself. If they loved gardening, buy some plants and plant them in your yard in their memory. If they loved to cook, make one of their favorite recipes. If they liked to hike, go take a long walk and think about them. When you're doing this activity, take a moment to share a memory if you're with other people, or think about a happy moment you experienced together.

Write Them a Card

I used to walk past the Mother's Day cards and wish I could buy one for Mom. One year, I'm not sure why, I felt called to buy my mom a card. I then went home and wrote her a letter. I told her everything I wanted her to know, in that letter, and it made me feel better to get it out. I don't even know what happened to that letter, but that isn't the point. It helped me feel connected to her, and I was able to release some of the feelings I was keeping inside. You don't necessarily have to buy a card, but get a piece of paper and write a note to your loved one. Tell them everything you wish you could say to them in person. Write about your life. Don't hold back. It might make you feel a little sad, but it will also make you feel good. You can keep what you wrote, throw it away, or even have a fire ceremony where you read it out loud and then toss it into the fire. This can be very powerful. Once, on a beach, I wrote my mom a long letter, put it into a bottle, and tossed it into the ocean. Don't judge. It was incredibly powerful and helped me to feel better. You might be surprised at how much you have to say once you start writing.

Talk about Them

Talking about your loved one, whenever you feel like it, and sharing lessons you learned or funny stories is a nice way to bring them into your life. Sharing past experiences and samples of their wisdom can help you feel connected to them and let other people know how much you love and miss them. I love sharing stories with my kids, and as my children have gotten older, when something they did triggered a memory, I didn't hesitate to share it.

Talk to Them

It might sound a little funny, but you can talk to your loved one, telling them whatever you want to say. You can do this through prayer, at night before you go to bed, or as you travel through your day. Do I think my mom can hear me? I would like to believe that she is watching over us, our guardian angel, smiling down on us and listening when we talk to her. Everyone is different, and I'm not about to tell you what to believe. I find this very comforting and I choose to believe she's with me, wrapping me in her love, whispering in my ear, watching over my family.

Visit Your Loved One

You can always go to the cemetery or the place where their remains were put to rest, and visit them. This can be comforting. Just sitting there and talking to them can help you feel like you're doing something with them. Take flowers, a special rock, or something you want to leave there as a way to mark your visit. At first, I was resistant to this idea, and it was difficult for me to see my mom's name written on her gravestone, just staring back at me. Over time, I've learned to feel better about being there.

One recent Thanksgiving holiday, when we were in Richmond, out of the blue my dad decided we were due to visit the cemetery. "It's been a while since we've gone to see your mom, and I think it would be a nice thing to do. Plus, the kids are getting older." Since he doesn't ask a lot of us, it was hard to say no. I wasn't excited about it.

"Dad wants us to all go to the cemetery tomorrow," I said to my brother, Ari, at our Thanksgiving dinner. I pulled him aside and tried to speak where no one else could hear us. He looked at me with a perplexed expression that said exactly how I was feeling.

"You're not going to say no," I said, being the older bossy big sister. "Dad expects us all to be there and we're going to be there." What I meant is that if I had to go, and drag my kids, he was going to go also.

"That's fine," my brother said, taking a deep breath. "We can do that."

We agreed to all meet at the cemetery the next day around noon, all twelve of us, at my mom's grave. Instead of Black Friday shopping, we were visiting our relatives in a cemetery. There we stood at the designated time, not sure what to do. We all felt awkward. We looked at one another, but didn't really say anything. I could tell my kids felt uneasy and uncomfortable. We needed someone to tell us what to do and why we were there. That's when my dad announced his plan.

"We're going to start at the oldest member of the family, go to that person's stone, and work our way back to Terri," he said. "Then we're going to say a prayer together. At each stone, let's share a nice story or memory of that person."

Having a plan made us feel more in control. We all followed my dad and walked to my great-grandmother's plot. My kids never met her and I barely remembered her, but family members shared beautiful stories about her, painting a picture of the woman she once was. In the Jewish religion, it is customary to leave a stone at a graveside to mark your visit. We saw many rocks on each of the headstones as we stopped by; it was nice to see that so many people had visited them. We added rocks to the graves of several family members, stopping along the way to remember other people we once knew.

We remembered happy times, shared memories, and tried to describe the people who had come before us so that our children would get a sense of who they were and what they meant to us. Instead of being stressful or stiff, the experience was relaxed and joyful, and it reminded us that family members came before us and will come after us.

One day, I hope that family members I'll never get to meet will visit my grave. I hope they'll feel a connection to me and my place in our family history. I understood that this is what my dad was hoping to teach his children and grandchildren.

As we finished the tour at my mom's graveside, my niece ran around chasing a butterfly and giggling, something I know my mom would have loved. Being there brought tears to my eyes, and I didn't hold back or try to stifle them. I let them roll down my face. I hope my mom was smiling down on us, happy that we were there, hearing the laughter of her granddaughter, and knowing how connected to her we remain.

CHAPTER 11

Letting Go of Perfectionism

My life isn't perfect, and I'm guessing yours isn't either. There are things in my past I wish hadn't happened—events I would like to do over or erase from my past. There are ups and downs, good moments and really challenging situations. But it's all part of the human experience. We live on a polarity planet, and we have to be willing to experience both poles. If you're lucky, by the end of your life you will have had more good moments than bad, but there aren't any guarantees. I've learned to accept this about life, and let go of my need to seek perfection. We learn from our mistakes if we give ourselves permission to take a step backwards and see what we might have done differently. Then maybe, if we find ourselves in a similar situation in the future, we can remember the lesson and make that situation a little bit easier for ourselves. Sometimes, when things didn't play out the way we wanted them to, there wasn't anything we could have done differently to change the outcome. Sometimes, just saying, "I did my best," *has* to be good enough. As much as I would like to, I can't control everything. Learning to let go and accept this, and roll with the uncertainty of life, trusting things usually work out, has helped me.

It takes a ton of time and energy to try to achieve the illusion of perfection. It's not that a little pressure is a bad thing. Working hard, persevering, trying to succeed, and going after our dreams, even if we have to regroup and figure out another way, are good things. But sometimes we can cross the line and head into dangerous territory. Trust me, I've crossed that line many times, and you don't want to go there. Try to be somewhere in the middle, in the space where it's okay to make mistakes and be human while living your life to the fullest. Get comfortable with failure, realize it's just part of life, and shut down your ego when it tells you, "I'm a failure for making a mistake." Blunders are part of growing. Learn from them, then get yourself back up and move forward. My friend Garth Callaghan, author of *Napkin Notes* and my podcast partner, is always telling me, "Dara, if you aren't failing, you aren't taking enough risks," and he's absolutely right.

Being judged by other people and feeling like you can never make them happy isn't a great place to be. You can't control what other people think, and if your happiness comes from their approval, you're basically giving them the keys to your soul. Sure, it feels good to get compliments and validation—I like that just as much as you probably do—but don't fall into the trap of relying on it. If you're only doing things to win people's approval, eventually you're going to lose. Maybe not right away, but you'll probably wake up one day and realize you were working so hard to impress other people that you might not even want what you have. You can only be fulfilled by other people's praise for so long. My mom and grandmothers didn't put a lot of unnecessary pressure on me to be perfect. They loved me for who I was, flaws and all, and not for what I accomplished. I know now that this was a gift. Don't measure your value by the opinions of other people. When you listen to the voice inside yourself and do things because they feel right to you instead of being dependent on what other people think, it's incredibly freeing. Give yourself permission to love yourself because of who you are, not what you've accomplished or the way other people see you. This is when the magic really happens. This is the place where personal growth, happiness, and joy are made.

As I write this in my pajamas on a Wednesday afternoon, I consider showering and getting dressed before Avi comes home from school; otherwise, this will be the third day in a row that she will come home to find me still wearing my PJs. If I jump in the shower now, I can get dressed before she comes home, and she'll never know. Then I remind myself that I'm embracing my authentic self and giving up the need to impress other people. If wearing my PJs and writing while listening to James Taylor makes me happy and is what I want to do, then good for me.

Sometimes, the things we don't like can't be changed, and our job is to figure out how to make peace with them. I wanted so much to change the fact that my mom passed away. But, eventually, I had to accept what happened. Similarly, I wanted to erase breast cancer from my past, but there's no way I could change what happened. We can only move forward, recognizing that we have the ability to make changes in our present life, if we're willing to do the work.

It can be painful to admit that we regret some of our past choices. Your goal is to get to a place where you can learn from your past, appreciate that you did the best you could at the time, and let yourself move forward. Take full responsibility for your life, own your past with all of your mistakes, and be honest about where you are. Then you can use this power for good and start making intentional decisions that are in line with what you want. Give yourself permission to admit you aren't perfect, and your relationships aren't perfect, and instead embrace the imperfections of life. You will probably be happier and more joyful and feel a lot less pressure and stress. As Maya Angelou once said, "Do the best you can until you know better. Then, when you know better, do better."

It's important to remember that no one is perfect and no relationship is perfect. I know that my mom and grandmothers weren't perfect. My mom was constantly late, ate really slowly, which was super frustrating, and sometimes had trouble sticking to deadlines. Grandma Millie and Grandma Margaret argued a lot and often put my mom in an impossible situation. Sometimes, little things became big deals and our lives became needlessly dramatic. We had little spats and didn't always bring out the best in one another. While I want to remember all the good times, the happy moments, I want to also acknowledge that my people were real people, just like me, and did the best they could with the hand they were dealt, just like I've tried to do. I try to remind myself of this when Zoe and Avi are pushing my buttons or we're arguing about something insignificant and meaningless.

I AM MY MOTHER'S DAUGHTER

PORTION OF A LETTER FROM MOM, 1986

*Dad and I are relaxing and getting a chance to enjoy life
together. Couples go through ups and downs, but when you love
each other you work through it. Your grandma and aunt are
still arguing over something. Who knows? If I didn't know better,
I would swear they acted like one year olds.*

Stay well and be happy!

Love, Mom

. . . .

If you grew up having a mom who was a perfectionist, she might
have transferred this impossible standard to you. If this is the case,
try to recognize it, forgive her, and realize that, going forward, you
have a choice. You get to decide how you want to live. You can give
yourself the freedom and space to learn, grow, and mess up. And if
you have a daughter, be intentional about how you parent her. History
doesn't have to repeat itself.

When Avi turned sixteen, we bought her a car. She and Jon
picked it up on a Saturday afternoon. That Sunday evening, she
had a group of friends over to study and couldn't wait to show them
her new car. It was dark when she took them out to look at it, but
they didn't care. The next morning as we pulled out of the garage in
my car, we realized that a back window of her new car had been left
open all night long, and it had rained. While the kids were sitting
in her car the night before, someone must have put the window
down and forgot to put it back up.

"You left the window down in your car, Avi," I said, "and you've
only had it for two days. Now the back seat is probably wet."

I was perturbed by her irresponsibility. If we were nice enough to get her a car, shouldn't she be able to take care of it? How hard was it to roll up the windows? Was this how she was going to take care of her most expensive item? And that's when she broke my heart.

"I'm sorry, Mom. I made a mistake," she said with tears in her eyes. "I'm not perfect and I didn't mean to let you down."

I never wanted to hear my child say those words. I've always told my kids that I make mistakes and so do they, and it's okay. I didn't say anything for a moment and just let her words sink in.

"Oh, Avi," I finally said, "you don't have to be perfect. Ever."

We talked the rest of the way to school. Later that evening, I brought it up again because her words had stung me so deeply, and I desperately wanted her to understand that she never had to be perfect for me to love her. I'm sure it's a conversation we'll continue to have, because our kids see what they perceive as perfection everywhere they look. The pressure they feel, and the standards they constantly measure themselves against, are too much for them. A seat in a car is easily dried, but damage to a child's self-esteem can last a lifetime. As a mom of daughters, I want to try and lessen the load they sometimes feel pressured to carry.

Our society, especially social media, bombards us with pictures of what a "perfect life" looks like; but it does not exist, just as there's no such thing as the "perfect" relationship, and you will never feel fulfilled if you're constantly searching for it. It's so empowering to realize this.

You might have had a mom who wasn't there, didn't parent you the way you needed to be parented, put a lot of pressure on you, judged you harshly, put you down, set unrealistic expectations, or was mean to you. The effects might have stayed with you as you grew up, and you might even hear unflattering words in your head—from her—that tore you down instead of building you up. Remember, you have a choice. Just as I had to decide to finally let go of the pain I had allowed to cling to me, you get to decide if you're going to stay in that space or release it and move forward. It's your life, your choice. Let yourself make it.

. . . .

WORDS OF WISDOM FROM MOM, 1982

Our dinner party was a complete success.
I was very organized and had everything under control.
I even set the table a day before. As a result,
I was not exhausted the night of the party.

I laughed at this when I read it, because even though this was probably written decades ago, it's still timely and relevant. It's all about finding a way to decrease the pressure we feel when it comes to fearing other people's judgments of us. Of course, she wanted her guests to have fun and feel welcomed, but she didn't want the cost to be her own enjoyment. My mom wanted to have everything under control ahead of time, so she could enjoy her party instead of running around trying to get it all done and feeling like things had to be perfect. Jon used to tell me when we had people over to our house that I turned into a crazy woman because I felt the pressure of being perfect. "Just enjoy yourself," Jon would tell me. "This is all for fun." Of course, he was right. Again.

If you are having a party, try to plan ahead of time, instead of waiting until the last minute to get all the details organized. You will enjoy your company so much more if you have everything under control and aren't exhausted the night of the party. I can attest to this, having done it both ways. My mom loved people; she loved being with her friends and family, and enjoying the time they had when they were together. You might even consider relaxing your standards a bit; you will probably have more fun.

Eating dinner together as a family has always been important to me, and something I grew up with. It was a priority while raising Zoe and Avi. Even when we were all super busy, we ate dinner together most nights. It was a way for us to connect with one another, if only for thirty minutes. We never knew where our conversation would take us, what topic would come up, and this kept life fun. All topics, serious or light, were okay. I hope Zoe and Avi look back on their childhood and remember having meaningful family dinners.

WORDS OF WISDOM FROM MOM, 1987

It is good to aspire to win, but it is important
to be satisfied with your best effort even if it is
not good enough to win or to be the best.
Honest and sincere effort is being a winner.

This is one of my favorite quotes from all the letters. It's a good reminder to acknowledge the journey, not just focus on the outcome in any given situation. How often do we try to accomplish something and then feel disappointed if the outcome is not what we had intended? When we focus on the outcome of a given situation, we miss a lot of the joy an experience can bring. Many of us think that, if we don't win, then we must be a loser. It's easy to see things in black and white. But there are a lot of shades of gray in life. Plus, life is a lot more fun when we let go of particular expectations and instead enjoy the journey, trusting that everything will work out well. I also learned that things can turn out so much better than expected.

The women in my family liked clothes and shopping and getting "all dolled up" for a holiday or celebration. Each year, before "Yontif," as Grandma Millie always called the holiday season of Rosh Hashanah, and before the Jewish New Year and Yom Kippur, the Day of Atonement, we always went shopping for a special holiday outfit. "You should always remember to have a new outfit for the holidays," my mom said, "to start the New Year off well and feel and look your best." It wasn't hard to convince me that this was a brilliant idea.

We had such fun on these outings, often going to lunch together, or stopping by a bakery and getting a sweet treat. It was a pleasant way for us to spend time together, laughing and having fun, while looking for "something special" to wear for the upcoming holiday. Grandma always gave me money to put towards my "Yontif outfit." It was generous of her, because I knew she didn't have a lot of "extra" money to spare. When Grandma Millie used to come and visit my family in North Carolina, we enjoyed taking her shopping and treating her. This made me so happy, and I loved getting to make her feel special. It warmed my heart to be able to spoil her a little bit, after all she did for me when I was growing up.

When my daughters were younger, I started this tradition with them, and always bought them a new outfit for the holidays. Sometimes, my mother-in-law, Suzy, and I would go shopping together and she bought them new outfits. They love clothes and shopping for clothes as much as I do, and we always have a lot of fun shopping together. I have a feeling that buying a new outfit each year to celebrate the Jewish New Year is a tradition my daughters will happily keep.

Establishing Your Own Family Traditions

I love traditions because they help connect us to our lineage and create special memories. If you're interested in starting your own traditions, it just takes a little thought and a bit of intention. It's never too late. Remember, it doesn't have to be complicated, expensive, or difficult. The purpose is to foster a sense of connection with your family, spend time together having a positive experience, and create beautiful memories. Here are several ideas to help you get started.

- Have a weekly family dinner such as "Meatless Monday," "Taco Tuesday," or "Waffle Wednesday." Everyone needs to eat, and you're probably going to cook anyway, so it's fun to turn this activity into a tradition. Plus, it will make your meal planning easier!

- A friend of mine plants a tree each time her family moves into a new house. They love the idea of putting roots into the ground and watching the tree grow as their family grows in their new environment.

- One of my friends gives her kids money every time they come home from college to visit, even if it's just for a night. "We call it relaunching money," she said. She and her husband fill her kids up with good food, lots of love, and also money. They seem to get plenty of visits, and I think this is brilliant. Hear that, Zoe and Avi? We have a new tradition.

- Holidays are a great time to look for ways to establish a ritual. I have a friend who takes his two daughters to lunch and a movie at the beginning of every holiday season. Then they go gift shopping together for their family. I know he looks forward to this special time with his daughters. Other friends have a certain meal they cook for a particular holiday, or family recipes they use to remind them of family members who have passed away.

- One of my friends loves to take annual family pictures wearing matching pajamas, and this has become a fun annual tradition. Plus, they have adorable pictures to hang in their home to remember this family practice.

🍃 I know a family who takes an annual trip to an apple farm each fall, with a picnic, and then they go home and bake pies together. It's just one day, but they do it each year, and have created many beautiful family memories of that apple farm.

CHAPTER 12

Letting Go of Things

I t's nice to be surrounded by things that once belonged to family members. I have many items in my house that belonged to my grandparents, Jon's grandparents, and my parents and in-laws. Furniture, clocks, pictures, art, and religious objects tend to pass from one generation to the next. I love having things in my home that trigger a memory every time I pass them. I keep a porcelain flower in my room, because it once sat on my mom's night table. I have a picture of a mother with her daughter that used to hang in the hallway when I was a child. I remember the day my parents bought this picture, at a temple art show, and how excited they were to hang it in our house. It's now in my dining room, and it makes me smile when I look at it. There are many objects around my home that I keep because they have a strong sentimental meaning to me.

But there can be a difficult side to keeping items that have been passed down to you. What if you have things that have been in your family for many generations, and you don't like them? Do you keep them or give them up? What do you do if the item triggers negative memories? Do you still keep it or do you let it go? I found myself in this situation, and I didn't even realize it.

When my mom passed away, most of her belongings were items she and my dad had owned together, and they stayed in their house with my dad. When he and Lois were married and moved into a new house, my dad offered many of them to me. "You don't have to keep them," he said, which I appreciated. But I realized that if I didn't keep the items, they would be donated to charity. Truth be told, I had trouble getting rid of anything that once belonged to my mom. I practically forced my dad to pack up many of her "special" clothes and put them in a storage closet in his new home. I couldn't bear the thought of getting rid of all of her clothes, especially the items that reminded me of happier times when I looked at them. There was the beautiful pink dress she wore to my wedding, the leather jacket she almost always wore with jeans, and several sweaters and coats that were "so her."

"Just pack up the special things," I pleaded, "and I'll go through them one time when I'm visiting. It's not like you don't have room, and it will be out of the way."

"Fine," my dad said. "But I'm not really sure why you're saving these things. What are you planning on doing with them?"

"I don't know," I said. "But I don't want to give them away."

He understood my need to hang on to a piece of her, and didn't push. Many times, on visits throughout the years, my dad would say, "You might want to go through the storage closet." It happened to be right next to the room that Jon and I stayed in when we were visiting.

"I'll do it next time," I almost always said. "When we have more time."

I struggled with the thought of getting rid of anything that had once been hers because I realized there was a finite number of belongings that were once hers. If we gave these things away, they couldn't be replaced. Once these items were gone, they were gone. Then, what would we have to remind us of her?

A set of clay statues made by my mom when she was sick ended up at my house when my dad and Lois moved into their new home. Each time I looked at the statues, they triggered a memory, but it wasn't a good memory. Instead of keeping them in a room I didn't often go into, storing them in a closet, or getting rid of them, somehow they stayed for sixteen years on a shelf in my den.

Soon after my mom was diagnosed with the stage four cancer, our family decided to purchase clay and pottery tools as a way to distract her. She needed something to do during the day that would take her mind off of her treatment plan and poor prognosis. She loved art, enjoyed making things with her hands, and clay seemed to be the solution. Truth be told, we needed to feel like we were doing something—anything. So we went shopping and bought art supplies. If you've watched someone you love fight a losing battle, you know how helpless it can make you feel.

I remember how excited she was when we came home from the art store and set up her art room with all the new supplies. She couldn't wait to start designing and creating. She wanted to make something for each member of our immediate family, and so my brother, my dad, and I each received a piece from her. Each sculpture was intended to represent where we were in our lives.

As I was pregnant with my first child at the time, my sculpture was of a mother holding her baby. My brother's was also a mom holding her child, and my dad's was a family of four, arms around one another. She didn't have a kiln or a way to glaze the designs, but they were taken by a friend and returned after being "cooked."

These statues were raw and ragged, earthy and fragile—a bit like my family as we held on to one another during this very difficult time in our lives. They didn't remind me of the vibrant woman I loved or the joy her life brought to those who knew her. Every time I passed the shelf, I recalled one of the saddest moments of my life. Yet it felt like these items were sacred and couldn't be removed.

It wasn't until I read about the importance of having things in your life that make you feel good and bring you joy that I even realized the effect these sculptures had on me. Once I realized this, I wanted them out of my house. It wasn't easy. What kind of person would give up something made for them with such love and care? What daughter would do such a thing? How could I get rid of sculptures made for me when my mom was dying? Hello, Jewish guilt, there you are again. Dammit.

Nevertheless, I was able to give myself permission to let go of them. I took a long walk alone and contemplated the three clay sculptures. I stood over the trash can in my kitchen, and I looked at each piece individually. I thought about my mom, and I silently explained to her why I was doing what I was doing. Then I pitched them into the garbage, one at a time, and watched them crumble into a thousand pieces. They broke easily. I didn't cry. I didn't feel sad. I felt relieved. I felt free. I quickly took the trash outside and went on with my day. What I learned from this experience is that it's okay to let go—of things, the past, whatever doesn't help you to be the best version of yourself. Even though it can be scary to release the old, it truly does open up space for us to bring in more of what speaks to our heart.

Now, I only keep items in my house that help me remember good moments with my loved ones, or that please me, even if I have no sentimental attachment to them. I am intentional about preserving the past and about honoring those who came before me, while making sure to nurture my soul. It took me a long time to get to this place, and I'm sure glad I did.

. . . .

LETTER FROM MOM, 1984

Dear Dara,

We hope you are having a nice time. At last I am finished with school. It is hard to believe that graduate school is almost over. I know that you and Ari will be glad when your Mom gets her nose out of the books. I too will be glad to be through. It has been difficult to study when I wanted to do so many things as a family. Without this master's degree I would be stuck professionally. I believe it is important to grow and to do new challenging things. You only live once. Dara you are in for a big surprise when you get home. Your room has been transformed!! I will say no more. We love you,

Mom
. . . .

. . . .

WORDS OF WISDOM FROM MOM, 1984

Each new experience opens your eyes
and broadens your horizons.

When we do new things and expose ourselves to unfamiliar peo-ple and situations, we grow. I don't know about you, but I don't want my life to ever feel stagnant or boring. Challenging ourselves and allowing ourselves to have new experiences is how we continue to keep our lives interesting and stimulating.

There are different seasons of life. Some seasons allow us more freedom to explore, and provide more time to do new things. In other seasons, we're just doing our best to juggle all of our respon-sibilities, and the thought of adding anything out of the ordinary to our "to do" list might push us over the edge. When Zoe and Avi were little and I was working, the last thing I had time for was add-ing more exciting undertakings to my life. But this doesn't mean there aren't ways to keep life feeling fresh and fun. It just means that in some seasons of your life you might have to work a little harder and be more intentional about how you spend your time. You can either find a way or an excuse.

Here are some ways to bring in a new experience even when you have a busy schedule:

- Try a different restaurant or order something you haven't tried at a restaurant you frequent. It's fun to go somewhere you have never been before and eat something other than your usual meal.
- Consider a new kind of exercise. If you usually take an exercise class, try a different class at your gym. If you normally walk outside, find a different route. Put a little thought into how you can add variety to your exercise.
- Mix up your schedule a little bit. Look for ways you can do what you need to do at a different time. This will help make your day less monotonous.

- It's fun to spend time with people other than your same "usual" crowd. Consider having a weekly or monthly coffee date or lunch with someone you would like to get to know a little better. I've been doing this since New Year's Eve, and it's been really fun. Sometimes, I click with the person and feel like a friendship is blooming; other times, I leave feeling glad I got to learn a little bit more about that person but knowing that was probably just a one-time thing. Get out of your comfort zone and reach out to someone new.

- Use the good china, the company towels, or whatever you've been saving for a "special" occasion. This will help make a normal day feel more special and give you a new experience.

- Rearrange the furniture in your house to make a room look completely different. A new candle, accent pillow, or blanket can also freshen things up a bit if moving your furniture around isn't an option. It's not just about bringing new items into your home; consider taking something out. Don't be afraid to take an honest look at the items in your house. If you don't like something or if it brings you down, let it go. And don't wait sixteen years before doing it.

- Open your eyes and pay attention. Really notice how you're living, your daily routine, who and what you surround yourself with, and try to see things objectively. Have the courage to make positive changes to help elevate your life and broaden your horizons. Level up your life by taking the time to have a life-edit.

When my Grandma Millie was really sick, and knew she was dying, there was a Saturday when she decided it was time to give away her jewelry. While she didn't have a lot of "extra" money, because my grandfather had owned a pawn shop back in the day, she did have a lot of jewelry. We all gathered at her house, and she enjoyed calling us into her room, one by one, and giving us her jewelry. She gave away her precious items, and even wanted to make sure she gave Lois several pieces as well. "Why should I wait until I'm dead?" she said. "I might as well enjoy giving you the items now so I can see how happy it makes you."

As a special gift, she had a beautiful ring made for me, and was so excited to give it to me that day. She handed it to me with such pride; she wanted to make sure I would always remember how special I was to her. The ring had a large diamond as the center stone, surrounded by very small diamonds. The center stone represents Grandma Millie, and each of the smaller stones signifies my mom, Aunt Shelli (my mom's sister), me, my cousin Bonni, and Zoe and Avi—all of "her girls." It is a treasure and very meaningful to me, and I am blessed to have it. When I wear it, I remember how much she loved me and our family. I can look at the stones in the ring and contemplate my place in this beautiful family.

I took the ring home with me and started wearing it.

"Are you enjoying the ring?" she would ask when we spoke on the phone.

"Yes," I would answer her. "Of course." I knew this made her very happy, and I could tell she felt proud.

"I'm so glad, Dara," she said. "You're a special girl and you should have a special ring."

"Tell me," she would say. "Did you get any compliments on the ring today?"

"Yes," I would say. "So many. Everyone loves it." I could imagine the smile on her face.

After a few weeks went by, she called me. "Dara," she said. "It seems like I'm going to live a little longer than expected. I hate to ask you this, but do you think you could bring the ring I gave you back to Richmond when you visit next? I want to enjoy wearing it and, then, when I die, you will get it back."

She said this very nonchalantly, and it was "so her." I laughed, and was happy to hear she still had her spunk. "Of course," I said, "I'll bring it with me this weekend when I come to visit." Sure enough, Grandma Millie lived many months longer, and got to enjoy wearing the ring.

We never had a conversation about her dying or not being here or what life would be like without her. This conversation is the closest we came to ever talking about her death. Sometimes, I wish I had talked to my mom or grandmothers about what my life would be like without them, seeking their advice or hearing the lessons they learned when they lost a parent. But I was always their child, and as with a lot of other families, death wasn't something we discussed.

CHAPTER 13

Writing a Letter
to Your Loved Ones

The bag of letters held the great gift of allowing me to "hear" the voices of my loved ones and get a fresh glimpse of their lives and personalities. I never thought I could feel so close again to my mom and grandmothers. The letters taught me that there is power in the written word, both in writing it and receiving it. For a letter writer, it feels good to sort through your thoughts about the recipient. For a recipient, it is good to know that someone cared enough about you to share their thoughts and feelings with you. I adore going to the mailbox and discovering an unexpected letter written to me. It brings me so much happiness, even if the letter is short. Though the convenience of technology has decreased the number of letters being sent, maybe after reading this book you will feel inspired to write a "real" letter.

There are different kinds of personal letters, including "just because" letters, "special occasion" letters, and "legacy" letters.

The "Just Because" Letter

Most of the letters in my ziplock bag fall into this category, and this is my favorite kind of letter to receive. Letters from my mom and grandmothers were about what was going on in their lives: daily events and plans for the future. When I read their letters, I can hear them talking to me; I can visualize them smiling or laughing. What I love most about their letters is how real they are. The writers weren't trying to impress me, and the letters weren't formally written. The writers didn't think too much about what they wanted to say. They had no agenda other than letting me know they were thinking about me. They told me how much I was loved, how proud of me they were, how they hoped I was having fun, and they gave me plenty of advice. They weren't concerned about spelling, grammar, punctuation, or crossed-out mistakes.

When you think about writing a "just because" letter to your loved one, remember that you don't have to wait for an important occasion. You can send a "just because" letter to a friend or family member to let them know your thoughts and to tell them you were thinking of them. I think you will enjoy writing a letter like this. There aren't any rules. Just write what feels good to you, about what's going on in your world and what you're up to. Be real, let your heart guide you, and have fun with it. If you make a mistake, don't worry about it. Remember, perfection isn't necessary.

Here's an example of a "just because" letter from Grandma Millie.

. . . .

"JUST BECAUSE" LETTER
FROM GRANDMA MILLIE, 1986

Dear Dara,

I know it has taken me a long time to write to you. Of course you must know that I have been at Virginia Beach for two weeks. Your mother, father, and Aunt Shelli were with me and I just loved it. We had such a good time together and it really was fun. Since Grandpa died, it was the first time we ladies were together and we really got along so well together. I know you are just having such a good time. What do you do every day? Who is your boyfriend? After all, such a pretty girl has got to have a beau. Your parents left two days ago to vacation and pick up Ari and I'm sure that by now you have seen them. Well, that's about all the news for now. Write real soon. Love you with all my heart,

Your grandmother, Millie

. . . .

The "Special Occasion" Letter

These are letters written and given at life-cycle events, such as a graduation from school, marriage, confirmation, the birth of a child, a Bat Mitzvah or christening, a birthday, or a holiday. Special occasions or big life moments often prompt the writer to say something meaningful to the recipient. Frequently, these letters talk about how happy and proud the writer is and what they hope for the recipient; they contain well wishes in a deeper, more intentional way than "just because" letters. Some people like to buy a card to mark specific occasions, and there isn't a shortage of Hallmark cards. You can buy a card for any kind of occasion. Many people spend a lot of time picking out a card because they are looking for the exact words to say to their loved one to mark the occasion, rather than writing the words themselves. I love getting cards like this, but I like it more when a person takes the time to write me a note in addition to the words on the card. When I receive a card that doesn't have any personal writing in it, except for "Love, X," I've noticed that I don't tend to save the card. Even if the person picked the card because these were the exact words they wanted to say to me, it doesn't feel personal. There's just something about handwritten words that feel more meaningful to me.

A friend of mine celebrates her wedding anniversary a month after her parents' wedding anniversary. For years, her parents sent her a store bought anniversary card saying, "To the Happy Couple." One year, instead of tossing the card, she saved it and then sent it back to her parents a month later, on their anniversary. Her parents kept the card when they received it, and sent it back to her the following year, adding the year and a few special words. This card went back and forth between them for years, until her parents moved out of their home and the card was lost. She shared this story with me years ago, and I loved it.

"Do you still send them a card?" I asked her when I was writing this book.

"Not anymore," she said. "But it was fun for a little while." I think she wishes they still had the card, but sadly, it was lost.

· ·

**BIRTHDAY CARD FROM MOM
ON MY FOURTEENTH BIRTHDAY, 1985**

Dear Dara,

*On this special day we think of the moment when you
entered our family. You have filled our lives with much joy.
You are an exciting person who has a great deal to give to
others. On your 14th birthday we wish for you happiness,
continued health and a positive attitude to make life
work for you. We will always support you, Dara,
and we shall always love you.*

Love, Mom
· · · · · · · ·

The "Legacy" Letter

They might not be your favorite, but these are important letters, written to be given when the writer passes away, and they often contain meaningful and heartfelt words that the writer wanted to say to the recipient. These are often the last words the writer will convey to the recipient.

When my mom passed away, the morning of her funeral my dad came into my room and gave me an envelope with a letter my mom had written to me.

"Mom instructed me to give this to you if she passed away."

"She did?" I said, very touched.

"There are three envelopes, for you, Ari, and me."

My mom wrote my letter when she was very sick, and it was only a few sentences. Sadly, I don't have the letter, but I will never forget what it said.

. . . .

LETTER FROM MOM, 1999
(THE DAY OF HER FUNERAL)

Please don't be mad at me. I tried my best and thought we were doing all the right things. At the funeral, handle yourself with respect and dignity. Always remember how much I love you.

Mom

. . . .

It made me sad to realize she had written this letter because she knew she was dying. She was worried I would feel like she had let me down, as if she could control the cancer taking over her body. It also made me realize how much she knew me. I was terrified to go to her funeral, and had even gotten a doctor to prescribe a few Xanax pills for me to take the morning of her funeral. Zoe was just a few weeks old, and life had dealt me a really hard hand. I did take a couple of those pills, and I don't regret it. Sometimes, a girl's just got to do what a girl's got to do.

Many years later, when my family met to go over Grandma Margaret's will, we learned there was a letter written by my grandfather, in the safe deposit box, to their sons, my dad and Uncle Jack. The letter indicated that if they were reading the letter, it would be because their parents had both passed away. My dad read the letter to us, and it was very meaningful. The letter was beautifully written, giving instructions, letting them know how proud my grandparents were of their sons, and how much they were loved. I imagine this letter had been written long before my grandfather passed away, with much thought and intention regarding what my grandparents wanted to say.

I learned two valuable lessons from this letter. First, it is better to write this kind of letter when you aren't sick and don't expect to pass away soon because you will probably be more capable of thinking about what you want to say; you'll be less emotional and better at communicating your thoughts. Second, it is incredible to receive such a letter from your loved one who has passed away; it's a meaningful gift you can leave to the people you love and care about.

I encourage anyone who is remotely interested in saying something to their loved ones upon their death to take the time to think through what they want to say and do it. Don't wait or get freaked out because you don't want to think about your death. Make it less about you, and more about what you want to say to the people who will be left behind when you pass away. Write words to your loved ones that will wrap them in your love and remind them how much you cherished them. It can be typed or handwritten. Though I prefer handwritten letters, there aren't any rules. The most important thing is that you write from your heart. I wrote a blog post containing a letter such as this to my daughters, and it is my most popular post. My website even crashed because it was shared so many times and it couldn't handle the traffic. Many people asked me if they could use my letter as a beginning, when writing their own letter, and you are welcome to use any part of it. I hope it helps you.

Here's an updated version of this letter.

. . . .

LETTER TO MY CHILDREN

It's strange to think that one day I won't be here with you. When I sit and think about this, it makes me sad. It's not something I think about often, because who wants to think about death? I'd rather spend my time living! However, I have things to say to you and I wanted to make sure you hear them. So, here we go:

1. *Remember the good moments: when we laughed so hard we cried, the fun we had being crazy and silly and just enjoying being together. Don't focus on the bad moments. When I yelled at you, it was because you needed to hear what I had to say. One day, you'll be a parent and then you'll understand.*

2. *Nothing is perfect in life: not you, not me, not our relationship. The same goes for your other relationships. If you're looking for perfection, you'll never be happy. Instead, look for the good in people. It's there.*

3. *The world is a beautiful place. Look for the beauty that's all around you, even in your darkest moments. Even when you don't think you're strong enough to handle something. Remember, I know you are.*

4. *Don't take anything for granted. Be grateful for what you have, and count your blessings instead of your problems. This is the secret to being the happiest version of yourself.*

5. *Spend money on things that speak to your heart, but remember that life is about the people in your life, not the things you have. It's fun to have nice stuff, but it's even better to have people to share your life with.*

6. *Don't fight over my jewelry. Seriously.*

7. *If Daddy gets remarried, be nice to his new wife. I'll always be your mom, but you have room in your life for a new friend.*

8. *The decision to marry someone is one of the biggest decisions of your life. Take it seriously, marry someone you trust and can count on, and marry for love. Find someone who will be willing to stay up with the baby, change diapers with you, and laugh even when times are hard.*

9. *Get a job you love so much that you forget it's work.*

10. *Surround yourself with people who make you feel good about yourself and who love and accept you for who you are. Ditch the rest. You don't need negative people in your life.*

11. *Be honest, always, but deliver the truth with kindness.*

12. *If I don't get to meet your children, tell them all about me. Every last juicy detail. Make sure you don't let my death get in the way of you living your life. I got stuck in my grief for a really long time after my mom passed away. Please learn from me. You can honor me by living each day of your life to the fullest. I hope you're listening with both ears. Get a counselor and do the work to move through grief. You can miss me and still be happy. I want this for you.*

13. *Treat yourself with kindness and respect and demand this from other people.*

14. *Don't do anything you don't want to do. Remember, happy people are beautiful.*

15. *Never take your health for granted and do everything you can do, on a daily basis, to be your healthiest, best version of yourself, mentally and physically. Each year, take a trip*

to a spa with one another, spending "sister time," and enjoy relaxing and being together. You know I love a good spa day. Have one for me!

16. *Cherish each other and be good to one another. There's nothing like a sibling. Be the best friends I raised you to be, and always have each other's backs.*

17. *Think of me when you see a beautiful sunrise or butterfly and know I'm always with you. Never forget how much you were loved. Always and forever.*

Love, Mom

If writing a letter like this feels overwhelming, don't rush through it. Instead, begin writing it, then step away from it and go back to it a week or so later. The most important thing is to think about what you really want to say to your loved ones. Remember that this letter will be the last thing you ever communicate to the recipient of the letter, and you want to make it as meaningful as possible. At the same time, let your personality shine through, and be yourself. If you're a serious person, write a serious letter. If you're a casual person, write a casual letter. Let the recipient hear your voice as he or she reads the letter. This is what will make it especially meaningful. By the way, if you aren't comfortable writing this kind of letter, that's absolutely okay also. Just do what feels good for you, and trust your instinct. Always, listen to your heart.

Here are a few topics you might want to consider, to help you get started, but you don't have to use these.

Topics to Consider When Writing a Legacy Letter

- Lessons I want you to remember
- Why I love you
- My favorite memories of times spent with you
- What I wish for you
- What I have learned from my life
- Why you make me so proud
- Advice I want you to have
- What I wish someone had told me
- How to make the most of your life
- Everything I want to make sure I tell you

If I were writing a "What I have learned from my life" letter, here's what I would say:

What I Have Learned from My Life

- Having a family I love being with is a true blessing.
- Good friends make life full and fun.
- I'd rather have less of something I love than a lot of something I don't like.
- Taking the time to organize in advance is way better than playing catch-up later on.
- People are more important than things.
- Going through something hard makes you stronger.
- Time is precious for everyone.
- Money can't make you happy, but it's way more fun to have it.

- It's always a good idea to have plans the day you get your hair cut.
- If you keep doing what you've always done, you're going to get what you've always gotten.
- My voice sounds really good when I sing in the shower. That doesn't mean I have a good voice.
- Binging on Netflix is a great way to spend a couple of hours, but don't overdo it.
- Helping other people actually makes me feel better.
- Worrying doesn't do anything but suck the joy out of life and ruin the present moment.
- Having a few bites of a really good dessert won't hurt anything.
- Just because something is hard doesn't mean I shouldn't do it.
- I learn a lot about myself when I travel somewhere new.
- I'll never regret spending time with my kids.
- Expect good things to happen because most of the time they do.
- Eating dark chocolate every day makes me happy. We should all find our chocolate and give ourselves permission to eat it.
- The size of a person's house doesn't equate to the size of their heart.
- It's better to do something because I want to do it, not so that I can say I've done it.
- I must be a good friend in order to have a good friend.
- Holiday shopping is better when I don't have to rush.
- Feeling jealous is a waste of energy.

- There's something really nice about a hot bath or a hot cup of tea.
- Staying in my PJs all day long doesn't mean I'm lazy.
- Doing a job I love feeds my soul.
- Happiness is a daily choice I make for myself.
- When I think I can, I'm usually right. When I think I can't, I'm usually right.
- Every day is a new opportunity to start over again.
- I'm not good at everything and it's okay. Focus on your strengths instead of your weaknesses.
- I feel better when I'm wearing a cute outfit.
- I don't like being around people who are grumpy.
- Exercising regularly makes me happier, healthier, and nicer to be around.
- Laughing until I cry feels amazing.
- It's not a great idea to wait until the car reads empty before going to the gas station.
- People who judge you aren't fun to be around.
- Your heart will never be too full to love someone deserving.
- Expectations can be a dangerous thing. Manage them.
- Living with gratitude and appreciating what I have brings me a lot of joy.
- The scariest times in my life have also been the times I've grown the most.
- Don't make decisions from a place of fear.
- When I try something and fail, I learn from the situation and then push myself forward and try again. Anyone can fail. Winners are the ones who aren't afraid of failure.

    📎 There's room for everyone to be successful.
         Celebrating my friends' successes doesn't diminish
         mine.
    📎 Life can be hard, but it's so very worth it.

You don't have to handwrite your letters, but I love seeing the handwriting of each of my relatives and holding something they once held in their hands because it deepens my connection with them. But there are no rules. The most important thing is to find a way to tell the people you care about how much they mean to you, in whatever way works best for you.

I admit, when I was writing this book, I had cards all over my house, stuffed into drawers or cabinets, that were given to me throughout the years. (This shouldn't be a surprise to you. Clearly, there is a pattern here!) Instead of keeping them in one place, a special place designated for important cards and meaningful letters, it was easier to just put a card into the closest drawer when I received it and forget about it.

Then I decided to stop writing and take the time to go all over my house, open up all the drawers, and gather all the cards I could find to see what I had in my possession. I was delighted to find lots of treasures and enjoyed reading through these, some from my daughters when they were very young, others given to me by family members and friends. I kept the letters and cards that meant something to me and designated a specific drawer in my night table for letters and cards going forward. Now, when I receive something meaningful and I want to keep it, I know exactly where to put it so that it won't be lost. I also know exactly what to do when I want to feel loved: I reread some of these beautiful letters and cards. I even tied pretty ribbons around some of the stacks of cards—making a pack of letters all from the same person. I've tried to find all the love letters Jon has given me over the years. Then I consolidated the letters and cards together, as I did with letters from the girls and other family members. These mean more to me than my most expensive belongings. As for the ziplock bag, the one that changed everything for me, it still remains right where it has always been: the top drawer in the wooden cabinet in my den. Safe and sound and always waiting for me to spend a quiet afternoon "hearing" my family members, whenever I want to spend time with them.

. . . .

WORDS OF WISDOM FROM MOM, 1982

Smile—Laugh—Do Things—Be Involved—
Sing—Dance—and Enjoy!

My mom really knew how to draw every beautiful morsel out of life, and enjoy each day. Sure, she had her own challenges and struggles, but most of the time she was smiling, laughing, trying to figure out a way to make the time to do the things she wanted to do, engaging in whatever situation she was in, and enjoying her present moment. She never met a stranger, and was one of the most fun loving people I've known. She always wore bright clothing, pinks and reds, and traveled through life with that vivacious energy.

Each day when you get up, try to think about the day ahead of you, how you can help yourself enjoy it more, and what you can do to make the most of it. Of course, not all of your days are going to be good days, and that's okay. If you do have a bad day, here's the great news: you get to wake up the next day and have a clean slate, a new day, another opportunity to start fresh. Remember, most of the time, your attitude will play a big part in this. Try to intentionally choose to do everything you can to help yourself feel happy, and move towards having a good day. Carrying gratitude with you each day will positively impact you and help you stay in a positive space. The less we think about ourselves and the more we think about how we can help other people, the happier I believe we will be. Try to do something nice for another person most days, and notice how your kindness comes back to you tenfold.

The Happiness Contract

It's your life, your choice, but happiness really is an inside job, and only you can find it for yourself. If you're ready to go after it, sign this contract, giving yourself permission to seek happiness and claim it for yourself.

I, _____,

promise, from this moment forward,
to do everything in my power to enjoy my
life. I believe I deserve this, even if I have
regrets, decisions I'm not proud of, or things
in my life I don't like. Regardless of what I'm
currently facing or what challenges I might
encounter in the future, I'm giving myself
permission to create a life that brings me joy,
contentment, and meaning. I can't change
the past; I can only move forward and I'm
determined to do just that. Happiness is a
choice, an attitude, and a mindset,
and I'm committed to creating it for myself,
today and every day.

Name: _____

Date: _____

Create a Happiness Drawer

Here's a fun way to help yourself get into the happiness zone, especially if you're having a hard day, which of course, we all have. Make a happiness drawer in your home, so you have a place to go when you need some serious nurturing. Let's say you have a really hard day, you come home, and you don't know what to do to help yourself feel better. Now, you have a plan: you visit your happiness drawer! Don't tell anyone in your family where it is. It's your secret stash. Here are a few items I recommend keeping on hand, but feel free to include whatever makes you happy: candles, your favorite candy or chocolate, delicious teas, fun magazines, a facial mask and some soothing lip balm, your favorite essential oil (mine is eucalyptus), and warm cozy socks and pajamas or loungewear that make you feel good when you wear them. You will love knowing this emergency kit is waiting for you if you need it, and when you do, it will be like receiving a big hug from your best friend—you. Don't forget to keep it fully stocked and ready to go. When you're out and about and find something you want to add to your secret stash, give yourself permission to buy it! You might want to keep a few meaningful letters written to you by your loved ones. This might just be the icing on the cake of your happiness drawer.

The members of my family tend to leave little notes for one another in the course of normal daily life. It's nice to get a random note when you aren't expecting it, and also fun to write one.

On one occasion I was about to go out of town, to a big speaking event, and I was a little nervous—okay, a lot nervous. It was a larger crowd than I'm used to speaking to, and I was pushing myself out of my comfort zone. I navigated through the airport and the three-hour flight, and finally made it to my hotel room. I was tired, but the adrenaline was pumping through my body. I was excited as I got into my room and start unpacking. As I opened my suitcase, I saw an index card right on top. Here's what it said: "I'm so proud of you and know it will go great. Remember how much I love you. Love, Jon"

There's nothing like traveling through your day and then receiving a beautiful and unexpected note from someone you love. This note made my day and helped me relax a little bit.

Complaining about doing something I didn't want to do one day, I decided I was going to say "no" to the ask, even though there would be people who didn't agree with my decision. However, I was questioning my decision, and as I cleaned my room and went into the bathroom, I found this note from Avi on a sticky note on my mirror: "Life is too short to do things you don't want to do. Today will be okay. I love you."

This unexpected goodie brought a huge smile to my face and reminded me that my decision was the right one to make. She had noticed.

When I first started my blog, Crazy Perfect Life, I was a little out of my comfort zone because I was putting my life "out there" and felt very vulnerable. Zoe wrote me this note and left it on my night table and I found it one night as I was getting into bed: "I am beyond lucky to have you in my world and I'm so proud to call you my mother."

I can't tell you how many of these notes I have, how many I've given to other people, and the incredible feeling it is to not only receive an unexpected note, but to also write one. Try it. You will like it!

Leaving little notes for the people you love has another benefit. It not only feels good to write them to someone you love, but they will probably enjoy getting then, and then might start writing you notes. This is how I ended up with all the little treasures I've gotten over the years. It is SO fun to do this, it doesn't take a lot of time, and it brings unexpected joy to the recipient.

CHAPTER 14

Start Your Own Sharing Journal

When I was little, I kept a journal that had a key so that I could lock it up and no one could read my deepest thoughts. I was especially concerned that my brother would break into my room, read my diary, and find out who I had a crush on. Through the years, I returned again and again to journal writing, and I'm so glad I did.

If you feel the slightest urge to start your own variation on the mommy-daughter journal, I encourage you to trust your gut and go for it. It's easy to start and I can't really think of a downside. This kind of journal can be done with your son or daughter, spouse, parent, close friend, or anyone you want to enhance your communication with. You can also set up a sharing journal between siblings, especially if you want your kids to grow their relationship with one another. It would have been a good tool to set up for my daughters a long time ago, but I never thought of it. A journal could have helped them work out some of their "sister drama" over the years in a healthy and constructive manner, leaving me out of it.

Try to keep it fun. Take it from me, it's really hard to write if you aren't in the mood. If you decide to set it up, allow yourself to be flexible and casual about how often you're going to write to one another and pass the journal back and forth. If you just let whatever is going to happen, happen, organically and authentically, and you don't have a lot of rules, you will probably be happier with the experience.

You can buy an expensive journal or use a plain notebook. You can also set up an online document and pass this back and forth if it feels better for you. I liked being able to take my journal into bed with me when I was getting ready to go to sleep, or to a coffee shop when I was in the mood. I'm more of a pen to paper kind of person, but you might prefer to do this online.

I wish I had thought of having a journal for each year, as my daughters grew. If you have young children, you might consider starting a yearly journal now or, say, at the start of each school year. Starting a journal when your child is young gets him or her used to sharing and working out issues in a constructive manner. It also improves their writing. Such a win-win all around! Plus, you will have a beautiful way to keep memories as your child grows.

You might be thinking, "How do I start?" First you figure out how you want to do it, either electronically or by using paper, and who you want to do this with. Then, you let the recipient know about your plan, and talk it through. It's important for everyone to be on the same page and to buy into the process. Lastly, you just start! Write about what you're thinking and feeling, what you want to say to the other person, or what you want them to know. It might feel awkward at first, but stick with it and you will find your groove. Try to write when you're in the mood, and make it something you look forward to doing, not a chore or yet another item on your "to do" list. My advice is to write from your heart. If you do this, you can't go wrong!

I gave Zoe a new mommy-daughter journal for her time away at school, but she hasn't sent it back to me yet. She would have to mail it, which would take extra time, money, and effort. And, let's face it, what college girl wants to have to deal with mailing something when she can just text me whatever she wants to tell me? While we talk often and text regularly, and I write her letters, it would be nice to have a journal between us. It is easier for people who see each other regularly to exchange a journal, but it could absolutely be mailed between people who live in different cities. It depends on the commitment level of the individuals involved. I'm still hoping to go to the mailbox one day and get a surprise package from Zoe containing the journal.

If you want some extra direction, here are some journal prompts to help get you started and get you in the flow:

- I was thinking about you and want you to know . . .
- I was thinking about you and was wondering . . .
- Here's what's going on in my life . . .
- I dream of . . .
- You mean so much to be because . . .
- Let's spend more time together doing . . .
- My day-to-day life is going . . .
- I am grateful for . . .
- What I love most about today is . . .
- I'm most excited about . . .
- What I love about you most is . . .
- You're amazing because . . .
- My favorite thing about you is . . .
- I'm proud of you because . . .
- I love watching you . . .

You can also maintain a journal just for yourself. I'm a big believer in the power of journaling, by hand, and have gained huge insights about my life while working out challenges through writing. I do believe that using pen and paper is better than using a computer, because there's something magical that happens when we write it out. It's easier to just write whatever stream of thought you're having; it feels freer, and there's less of an urge to edit as you go. But if you'd rather use a computer, go for it. I keep a small personal journal with me almost all the time, and even take it along when I leave my house. This way, I can write when I feel called to do so. I've sat in waiting rooms, doctor's offices, and coffee shops, writing away. I try to give myself a little journal time every day. Again, do what works for you, and keep it as simple as possible.

I like to start my daily journaling by listing several things I'm grateful for. This helps me connect with my inner thoughts and get into the gratitude space. Try to write about what you're thinking and feeling. This isn't about what you did today or yesterday; it's about any insights you have gained. It doesn't have to be perfect. No one is going to read it but you. In fact, I don't even keep my journals. Some people like to go back and reread their journal entries, but I shred mine or toss them in the fireplace when all of the pages have been used (don't tell Jon.) Many people like to journal first thing in the morning, to start off their day in a relaxed manner, or before they go to bed, to release anything from the day, or both. If you stick with it, you will find your groove.

Here are ten journal prompts to get you started:

- 🍃 I feel happiest when . . .
- 🍃 I want the following from my life . . .

- To live an authentic life, I would need to do . . .
- Dear future me, here's what I want you to know . . .
- Dear past me, here's what I want you to know . . .
- The dreams I have for myself are . . .
- I'm scared of . . .
- On a day-to-day basis I feel. . . . I want to feel . . .
- Changes I want to make in my life are . . .
- What I love about my life the most is . . .

In this day and age, we're very blessed to have many different and easy ways to communicate with the people we care about, besides writing letters and having a journal. With technology, it gets easier and easier to keep in touch with the people we care about, even if we don't live in the same geographic location.

LETTER FROM MOM, 1986

Dear Dara,

Hi—this is your mother writing you. Do you remember me? Tell us about camp. We want to hear something! All is well at home. My days are spent working in the house, organizing, working out at the Spa, walking with your dad and playing a little tennis. Let me tell you, this is the life. But 2 people are missing to make things just right. You and Ari make everything we do more fun. Stay well, and let me know how you are!

Love, Mom

Here are several other ways you can connect with the people you care about, and grow your relationships.

- ✐ *Video:* You can always hit the "record" button on your phone and make a fun video with a special message. This way the recipient can hear your voice, see you, and receive your message. Plus, you can just hit the "send" button on your phone and the recipient can watch the video whenever he or she wants to watch it.
- ✐ *Social media:* This is one of the easiest ways to stay connected to people, in a fast and simple manner. Just leave a nice comment on someone's social media post, and let them know you're thinking about them. It's an especially beautiful way to keep up with past school or camp friends, previous work colleagues, or acquaintances. This is also a great way to stay connected to new friends and learn more about one another.
- ✐ *Email:* It's fast and easy to send an email letting someone know you're thinking about him or her. Just make sure, if you receive a meaningful email and you want to keep it, that you print it out or save it in a special place. I lost the second page to the email my mom sent to me after our trip to Alaska, because we got rid of that computer and I wasn't careful about saving the email. You can set up folders on your computer to keep special emails you receive, to ensure that you don't accidentally lose something meaningful, or else back it up.
- ✐ *Napkin notes:* My podcast partner, Garth Callaghan, author of *Napkin Notes*, is a big believer in the power

of taking a napkin and writing a note when packing lunch for your child. This is such a beautiful way to let your child know you're thinking about him or her. And, as I shared with you above, it doesn't have to be a note on a napkin. I love writing little notes to my family, and putting them on the car seat, in a suitcase, on a bathroom mirror, or wherever it will be an unexpected surprise for them when they find it. I enjoy doing this when I'm leaving someone's house, because it's fun for them to find it much later.

- *Voice transmission:* You can easily hit "record" on your phone and send someone a nice message. I have a friend who does this each morning with another friend. I don't think they save all of these messages, but they love hearing from one another, and they can do it when it works for their individual schedules. This is especially great if you're in a different time zone but want to actually hear the voice of your friend or family member.

- *Pictures/scrapbooks:* Oldies but goodies! Pictures are always fun to send, electronically or through the mail. I love that social media lets people keep up with pictures. I find I don't actually print out pictures like I used to do because I have the pictures on my phone or social media account. Every once in a while, save your pictures and even back them up, because you don't want anything to happen to them if your phone dies.

Here are other ways you can connect with the people you care about without having a keepsake:

FaceTime: It's fun to FaceTime someone and see him or her while you're talking. It's especially great if you want to show the other person something and you aren't in the same location. Now that Zoe is in college, she tends to FaceTime me in the morning while she's putting on her makeup. It's a fun way for us to connect, stay in one another's lives, and see each other. This is a great way for people to "see" their loved ones, especially if they're far away. It makes missing your loved one feel a little less painful.

Phone calls: I always love hearing the voices of my friends and family, and the telephone is still one of my favorite ways to keep in touch with people. When you talk with someone, you don't just exchange words, you're able to get a handle on their emotional state and where they're coming from, and you can be in your PJ's while you're doing it. Clearly, I'm showing my age! If you have older parents and grandparents, I'm fairly sure this is their preferred way of staying in touch.

Texting: I love how easy it is to send a quick message via texting, especially if I'm trying to coordinate plans with a lot of people, share something with everyone in my family at one time, and communicate details. But I personally don't believe this is a great tool for serious or meaningful exchanges. Plus, most people don't save their text messages for prosperity. However, if you have teenagers, this is a great way to communicate with them. In fact, having a teenage daughter and another daughter in college, I'm incredibly thankful for this tool. That way I don't have to send a letter like the one my mom sent above, and teenagers are pretty good about responding and letting you know they're okay.

. . . .

WORDS OF WISDOM FROM MOM, 1984

Seeing, exploring and learning broadens you so much and provides you with many good memories.

We're never too old to see, explore, and learn, and this is how we continue to grow. I love hearing about someone in his or her sixties or seventies who is back in school, traveling the world, or discovering a previously hidden talent. This world is full of incredibly beautiful sights and places and things to fall in love with. Don't ever think you're "too old for that," because you aren't. Age really is an attitude. You can set limits on yourself or you can commit to exposing yourself to as much as possible and creating joyful moments for yourself. As for me, what I've learned through all that I've seen and been through is not to wait until I have the "perfect" moment to follow my dreams or go after something. I've seen many people wait for the "perfect" moment to do something, and guess what? Too often they don't get to do whatever it is they wanted to do. You can find a way or look for an excuse. It's really all about what you're willing to do. Just don't let fear get in the way or shut down your dreams. It's incredible what happens when you grow up being told you can be whatever you want to be or do whatever you want to do. A funny thing happens. You believe it. You think you can absolutely do whatever it is you dream of doing. Let go of any limits you or someone else has placed on you, release any stories you might be telling yourself about why you *can't* do something, and go for it.

This is also how we continue to make beautiful memories. Allow yourself to be stimulated, broaden your horizons, and try new things. If you are bored, if you feel like life has gotten stagnant, and you don't know what to do, really think about what excites you, and then have the courage to bring that into your life. The most important thing is to make as many good memories as you can, love the people you are blessed to have in your life, and make the most of the time you have.

I was having lunch with a close friend when she told me it was the twentieth anniversary of her daughter's death.

"It's hard to believe it's been almost twenty years," she said. "In some ways it seems like a lot of time but in other ways it feels like it's just been a few years."

I nodded my head because I completely understood what she was saying.

"I'm so thankful for the journal you gave me when she passed away and that I have it now."

We were eating lunch and I paused because I had no idea what she was talking about.

"I gave you a journal?" I said.

"Yes," she said, "and I've been writing in it each year, on the anniversary of her death."

"You have?" I said. I was intrigued.

"It has been very healing to write to her and connect with her on the pages of the journal. I tell her how much I miss her but also news from the year and what I'm grateful for. I look forward to writing to her each year. I also take the time to reread the whole journal every year on the anniversary of her death. As I build up to her anniversary and face all the emotions, the sadness and dread of the day, it is a relief and a release to put it all in the journal. It helps me move on and feel grateful again."

I was stunned. I've known this friend for over twenty-five years, and we talk about almost everything, but we never talked about this before. I didn't remember giving her this journal. She lost her daughter the same year my mom passed away and there was a lot of sadness to process. I'm sure there's a lot I don't remember from that year, twenty years ago.

"I'm so glad you did this," I said. "What an incredible idea."

"I keep it in my night table," she said. "And I like having it right there. It helps me feel more connected to her."

I had never thought about keeping a journal specifically for writing to my mom, or to someone who had passed away. This was a different form of the mother-daughter journal and I thought it was a beautiful idea. The conversation also showed me that we can all learn from one another, and I hope this book helps people do just that.

CHAPTER 15

Living All Through
the Lens of Love

When I think about the experience of finding the mommy-daughter journals and reading the bag of letters, I can't help but get a little choked up. It's easy to get distracted by the demands of daily life, but this experience helped me remember what matters most to me. I know there is nothing more important to me than my family and the people I'm blessed to share my life with. I also understand that a life well lived is one in which we experience all the emotions, from pure joy to deep sorrow. We don't get one without the other.

· ·

PORTION OF A LETTER FROM MOM, 1992
(MY TWENTY-FIRST BIRTHDAY)

Dara,

It's hard for me to believe that you are all grown up—21. It seems like yesterday that you were a baby. I have watched you grow

*into a lovely young woman. I am very proud of you and hope
that most of your life will be filled with happiness and joy. Love
life, and make each day so special that you see the beauty and
smell the roses.*

Love, Mom

Going back and thinking about my past, I see how my mom's death, over twenty years ago, affected everything that happened from that moment on. There are people who will read this book and think, "Her mom died—why couldn't she just get over it?" or, "Everyone will die one day—why did she let her mom's death have so much power in her life?" or, "Why didn't she turn to God and trust that whatever happened, happened for a reason?"

These are valid questions that I never asked myself until now. Until writing this book. Until taking an honest look at my life. Sometimes, when you're in the middle of living, it's hard to get a big-picture view of your situation. We get wiser with age, gain insights our younger selves didn't have, and learn from life experiences. I can look back on the past twenty years and, if I'm being really honest, see the negative impact my mom's death had on my daily life. Something I know my mom would be very sad to learn. But I also know I can't go back. All I can do is accept what was, give myself a dose of strong love, and remind myself that I did the best I could at the time.

If I could go back, I would allow myself to feel all the feelings, and I would also tell myself that I had a choice: to move forward or to stay stuck. Maybe, if I had known the positive impact that reading the letters would have on me, I could have read them and been reminded of my mom's desire for me to make the most of each day of my life. Her words might have inspired me to get on with the business of living. I would have been more intentional about seeking out help, leaning into self-care, and pulling myself out of the pain. Reading words from my mom and grandmothers saying they wanted me to be happy, just as I want Zoe and Avi to be happy one day when I'm no longer living, probably would have been the push I needed to move through the pain and sorrow.

I was blessed to have a good relationship with my mom and grandmothers, but I recognize that there will be people who read this book and think, "Not everyone has the kind of relationship you had," or, "Your relationships were positive, but many people don't have good relationships with their family members." I understand this. Again, it comes back to acceptance of your circumstances and awareness that you have the power to change things.

First, you have to take an honest look at your relationships and be willing to see where you stand. Second, if you don't have good relationships with your family members, you can try and strengthen your relationships, if this is important to you. If you haven't had good relationships with your family members, here's the thing: you'll never know until you try. If it were me, I think I would risk feeling vulnerable and getting hurt to try and mend those relationships. But it's your life, your choice. Just remember that you might not get another chance.

By the way, you might have to forgive a loved one for their past transgressions. No one is perfect and no relationship is perfect. Life is too short to carry a grudge, hold on to pain, or refuse to give someone another shot. People change, time and life experiences tend to soften the edges a bit, and you might find your loved one is different in this season of his or her life. Every relationship is unique, though, and you will have to decide for yourself. If it's important to you, you'll do it. Just remember that time is precious, the future is unknown, and you don't want to have regrets.

Not a day goes by that I don't think of my mom and grandmothers. I will always miss them. There's a void in my heart that only they can fill. My grief has changed over the years, as time has passed and I've grown, but it is still there, as I imagine it always will be. Now, though, the pain has lessened as I've learned to focus on the positive. I know they are forever with me, wrapping me in their love, whispering advice, and watching over me. I hear their words and their laughter; I remember their smiles and the way they held my hand; I sometimes feel their presence. We are forever bound together by our deep love for one another. They taught me to love, led by example, and showered me with wisdom.

I am my mother's daughter, and Millie and Margaret's granddaughter, just as Zoe and Avi are my daughters, my mother's granddaughters, and Millie and Margaret's great granddaughters. We are forever linked, one woman to another, one generation to the next. Our place in our family's history is marked by the love we share, how we treat one another, what we pass on to future generations, and the lens of love through which we see.

. . . .

WORDS OF WISDOM FROM MOM, 1993

It seems to me our relationship enlarged
to include a friendship between us based on common
interests and compatibility. You are my friend,
one that I will always deeply cherish.

As I got older, graduated from college, and got married, my relationship with my mom turned into more of a friendship. She was still my mom, and mothered me, and there were topics I would only tell my girlfriends, but our relationship evolved into a beautiful friendship. We weren't living together and this actually helped us grow closer. She wasn't nagging me about "taking my stuff upstairs" or "cleaning my room." Instead, my mom became a trusted friend I could turn to for advice, and I knew she always had my best interest at heart. She didn't tell me what to do, but her opinion mattered a lot to me. Sometimes, she turned to me for my opinion on a given topic, and I was more than happy to share my thoughts. This probably would have continued as we both got older. I never got to see my mom become an older woman, and I think about this sometimes, but I've accepted it.

When I was younger, my mom was my mom, not my friend, and I tried to remind myself of this when I became a mom. I knew my daughters didn't need another friend; they had plenty of those. Instead, they needed a mom. They needed me to parent them, as hard as it was sometimes, at various seasons of their lives. There were times when I felt the burden of this responsibility, knowing the impact of my decisions. As my daughters grow and mature, I imagine our relationships will continue to become more like loving friendships. I can start to see this a little bit, and it's something I cherish. Spending time together will always be a priority for me, and I hope for them.

The relationship between a mother and daughter is precious and sacred, and one I value with all my heart. If you're blessed to be a mother, recognize how lucky you are. If you're blessed to be a daughter, recognize how lucky you are. If you're blessed to be both, recognize how lucky you are. There's a special connection we have, as women, to pass on family stories and wisdom from one generation to the next. We have the power to impact the lives of our loved ones and of future family members we will never meet. Let us be worthy of this power, intentional with our interactions, and loving. For in the end, love is really all that matters.

It was winter break, school was out, and our family went away for a few days. It was nice to all be together again. Even though the girls had their own hotel room, we somehow ended up in their room one night after dinner, piled up on Avi's bed, snuggling up and laughing, watching a movie. It felt like old times, when the girls were younger. After the movie, we all just stayed where we were. No one wanted to move.

"I just love our little family," Zoe said.

"It really is the best," Avi chimed in.

Jon grabbed my hand and squeezed it. We looked at each other and a smile passed between us.

We've made mistakes. We haven't been perfect parents. I'm sure there are things we could have done better. But through it all, the four of us have loved one another so much, and this means everything to me. I know that things will change. The girls will have their own family units one day and, God willing, have their own children and maybe even daughters. In a short time, Jon and I will be empty nesters. If we're lucky, one day we'll be grandparents. But I hope my daughters know this nest will always be there for them, a place for them to land where they can count on unconditional love and support. A place to always come home to. Life goes on, time passes, but it's in these precious family moments that I feel my mom's presence and hear her words, "Love one another. Take care of each other." And that's exactly what I'm trying to do.

ABOUT THE AUTHOR

W hen Dara Kurtz was twenty-eight years old, her mother died of cancer—a devastating loss that was compounded years later by the loss of both of her grandmothers. She sorely missed talking to them and getting their advice. Yet for decades, Dara had kept their letters to her hidden in the bottom of a drawer, fearful that rereading them might be too painful. One day, longing for contact with these women who had loved and raised her, she did reread their letters, which brought back beautiful family memories and taught her many life lessons. They caused her to reflect on the priceless love between mothers and daughters and how wisdom and traditions can be passed on from one generation to the next. Reading the letters brought Dara unexpected peace and a sense of connection to the family she misses.

Six years ago, when Dara was forty-two, her life seemed to be going brilliantly, with her loving husband, Jon, their daughters, Zoe and Avi, and her successful career as a financial advisor. Then she was diagnosed with breast cancer. Luckily, the cancer was found early, she went through aggressive treatment with surgery, chemo, and radiation therapy, and is blessed to be on this side of it. During this ordeal, Dara longed to talk to her mother and grandmothers, and thought a lot about her mortality. What she once thought important didn't seem so important anymore. She questioned her life choices, including her career. Having lost interest in balance sheets and financial statements, she quit her job at a large bank and decided to start her blog *Crazy Perfect Life*.

In her speeches, blog, podcasts, and writings, Dara shares funny, inspirational, real life stories, as well as tips and information to help others strengthen their relationships and find joy in their perfectly imperfect lives. Today her personal blog, *Crazy Perfect Life* (www.crazyperfectlife.com), reaches over 180,000 followers. Dara is the author of two books, *Crush Cancer: Personal Enlightenment from a Cancer Survivor* and *Crush Cancer Workbook*.

You can follow Dara Kurtz on social media and on her podcast.

Social Media: Facebook: @crazyperfectlife,
Instagram: @crazyperflife, Twitter: @crazyperflife
Podcast: Thrive: The Podcast with Garth and Dara. Part of life is facing and overcoming challenges. This podcast helps listeners overcome whatever challenges they might encounter.

Dara Kurtz is a popular speaker at medical centers, Jewish community centers, and women's organizations, and she also leads workshops. Popular among her topics are:

- How to Strengthen Your Relationships from One Generation to the Next.
- Are You My Friend or My Mother? The Mother-Daughter Relationship.
- How to Survive the Loss of a Loved One and Move Forward Physically and Emotionally: Tools for Finding Peace and Understanding.
- The Importance of Writing Love Letters to the People You Care About: The Benefits of the Handwritten Word.
- Are You Living the Life You Truly Want to be Living? Tips and Tools to Examine Your Relationships, Purpose, Community Connection, Health and Wellness, and Spirituality.
- How to Empower Yourself After a Cancer Diagnosis, Release the Fear, and Regain Control Over Your Life and Move Forward.

Interested parties can reach Dara at dara@crazyperfectlife.com.

DISCUSSION QUESTIONS FOR BOOK
CLUBS AND READERS' GROUPS

1. How can individuals find out more about their family history and about family members they never met? Is this important?
2. What would you like future generations to remember about you?
3. Is there anything our society can do better to handle the reality of death?
4. If you have lost a loved one, have you done your "grief work?" If not, what can you do to help yourself move through the pain? What did you learn from the experience of grief that might help you in the future?
5. How can you help other people deal with their losses?
6. Is it possible to maintain a relationship with someone who has passed away? How?
7. What might you do to strengthen your relationships and connect more with the people in your life?
8. Identify one person you would like to grow closer to. What can you do to make this happen?
7. The mother-daughter relationship can be challenging, especially during the daughter's teenage years. What can mothers and daughters do to help one another during this time?
8. Would you consider writing a legacy letter? How would you start?
9. Would you find it useful to keep a sharing journal? How would you begin?
10. Dara is a big believer in the importance of daily self-care. Share some of your favorite self-care practices.